Calm Amid The Chaos

A Practical Guide To Cope With Stress That Will Reduce The Chaos In Your Life

Miranda Yates

© **Copyright 2021 - All rights reserved.**

The content contained within this book may not be reproduced, duplicated or transmitted without direct written permission from the author or the publisher.

Under no circumstances will any blame or legal responsibility be held against the publisher, or author, for any damages, reparation, or monetary loss due to the information contained within this book, either directly or indirectly.

Legal Notice:

This book is copyright protected. It is only for personal use. You cannot amend, distribute, sell, use, quote or paraphrase any part, or the content within this book, without the consent of the author or publisher.

Disclaimer Notice:

Please note the information contained within this document is for educational and entertainment purposes only. All effort has been executed to present accurate, up to date, reliable, complete information. No warranties of any kind are declared or implied. Readers acknowledge that the author is not engaged in the rendering of legal, financial, medical or professional advice. The content within this book has been derived from various sources. Please consult a licensed professional before attempting any techniques outlined in this book.

By reading this document, the reader agrees that under no circumstances is the author responsible for any losses, direct or indirect, that are incurred as a result of the use of the information contained within this document, including, but not limited to, errors, omissions, or inaccuracies.

Table of Contents

Introduction vi

Chapter 1: What Is Stress and Why Do We Feel It? 11

    What Is Stress? 12

Chapter 2: Stress Triggers, Signs, and Symptoms 27

    What Are Stress Triggers? 28

    How to Recognize and Deal With Stress Triggers 55

Chapter 3: The Role of Stress in Our Lives 58

    Why Do Living Things Experience Stress? 60

    Types of Stress 61

    Identify Stressors in Your Life 63

    Is All Stress Harmful to Us? 68

Chapter 4: The Physical Manifestation of Stress .. 83

    How Does Stress Impact the Body? 85

Chapter 5: Exhaustion, Burnout, and Fatigue—How to Recharge Your Batteries 103

    What Is Burnout? 104

    Why Do We Feel Burnout? 112

    How to Deal With Burnout and Emotional Fatigue 115

Chapter 6: How to Stop Stress In Its Tracks 126

The 10 Things to Stop Stress In Its Tracks 127

Chapter 7: Cook Up a Stress-Free Life 135

Does Food Affect Our Mental Health? 136

Chapter 8: Simple Ways to Relieve Anxiety and Stress 148

The 20 Simple Ways You Can Reduce Stress 150

Chapter 9: Scientifically Proven Stress-Relief Techniques 157

Medically Endorsed Stress-Management Techniques 158

Fast-Acting Stress-Management Techniques 162

Conclusion 165

References 168

Introduction

Picture these familiar scenarios. Maybe you can relate to these:

You're at work and ready to get started for the day. From the minute you walk inside your office, you're bombarded with emails, memos, and reminders about the big project that is due today. You know your team is behind on the work and needs to catch up ASAP, otherwise, you're all on the chopping block. Your team is relying on you to get the job done and so is your boss. On top of all that, you need to manage your day-to-day tasks as well along with the project.

Your stomach seems to be in knots. You have a severe headache and it's only 10 p.m. You need to figure out how to get through the rest of the day, complete the tasks, and hand in your project. You're feeling like a short-tempered person and guzzling coffee by the hour. You just need to get through today; you grit your teeth and soldier on. It has to be done.

Maybe this is more relatable to you:

You wake up at the crack of dawn to the sound of a screaming kid. Eyes blurry, you shuffle out of bed and make a bottle for your screaming baby. Giving the baby the bottle, you quickly run to the bathroom. The moment you close the door, you hear screaming again. You sigh: This needs to be managed.

After half an hour of trying to soothe the fussy baby, it's time to wake your other kids up for school. You gently try to wake up your daughter who kicks you and turns over. Your son wakes up crying that he has a stomachache and does not want to go to school. He does this every day. You drag the blankets off both your children and coax them up.

With the baby in one hand, you run around the house like a headless chicken, trying to gather your children's belongings, get them ready for school, and serve them breakfast. You're doing everything to make sure your children make it to school on time while trying to ignore the cacophony of whining kids and screaming babies in your ears.

When the kids are finally on their school bus and the baby asleep, you sink into your chair trembling, every bone in your body aches from exhaustion. It's only 8 a.m. You have an entire day of cleaning and cooking to get through before the kids come back home from school. Then, you have to do this all over again.

Maybe this is more familiar:

Your final exams are just a week away. You've been pulling more all-nighters than you ever have in your life, and more often than not, you find yourself waking up in the library. You have to hand in three assignment submissions to complete your module this semester, otherwise, you would have to stay in college over the summer to make up for it. You can't afford to do that. You've been studying and working nonstop, and you're drained. The only thing that's keeping you going is the thought of going home over summer break. If you fail this module, you won't be able to do that and have to stay back over the summer.

You're trying to manage work on top of your studies so that you can support yourself through college. Your workplace doesn't care that it's your finals, so after studying the entire night, you have to put on your apron and head down to the coffee shop where you work as a barista, and you have the morning shift.

You're so stressed that you sometimes forget where you are and what you were meant to be doing for a minute, and then it comes back to you. You're mixing up your customer's orders because you just can't remember what they asked for. Snippets of your assignment keep floating in your mind.

You feel like a sleep-deprived student. The little sleep you do get is plagued by nightmares. You can't wait for this term to end so you can go home and sleep.

If any of the scenarios mentioned above seem relatable to you, know that you're not alone. Even if they don't apply to you, we all have different causes of stress in our lives that ruin our mental peace.

If you've picked up this book, it's evident that you're looking for ways to make your life less stressful and more carefree. Well, you've made the right decision. Through this book, you can learn more about stress and figure out how you can get rid of stress from your life.

You will learn what stress is and the different types of stress. You might be surprised to learn that not all stress is bad. You will understand the difference between good stress and bad stress after reading this book.

This book will help you identify your stress triggers and give you coping mechanisms so you can better manage your stress. It also offers scientifically proven stress-management techniques that you can incorporate into your life to handle your stress better.

If you're feeling mentally drained, physically exhausted, and overall just fatigued, this book will help you identify the reasons why and tell you how to improve the situation. Stress can manifest both mentally and physically, taking a serious toll on your health. This book will show you how you can alleviate that stress through a myriad of techniques focusing on your mental health, physical health, and even your nutrition. You'll be surprised to learn how stress can sneak into facets of your life that you never even imagined. This book will help you identify those stressors and get you started on your journey toward leading a carefree life.

Imagine living life without a care in the world where you don't have any overwhelming stress or anxiety, and you have the tools to stop such negativity in its tracks. This is not some Utopian dream.

It's possible, and this book will show you how. Welcome to the first day of your new carefree life.

Enjoy!

Chapter 1:

What Is Stress and Why Do We Feel It?

Every living thing on this planet experiences stress. From humans to animals and even plants to single-cell organisms, we all can feel stress. But what is stress? Why do we feel stressed? What are the factors that lead us to experience these feelings?

Let's find out.

What Is Stress?

The term "stress" as we understand it is our natural inability to deal with certain demands, events, or stimuli in our lives. Stress in some ways can be good for us, but if we constantly feel like we are in a state of stress, it becomes a chronic condition that is difficult to manage and can negatively impact our quality of life.

We all feel stress for different reasons. Animals in the wild can feel stressed if they are threatened or cannot find enough food. We feel stressed if we are under pressure either at work, school, in our relationships, or when we're dealing with money. Anything that challenges our view of the world or becomes an obstacle in our effort to live a comfortable life can become a source of stress. If we feel like our well-being and peace of mind is being threatened, we can respond to that with stress.

When we feel stressed, the "fight-or-flight" response our bodies naturally have gets triggered. This response is our instinctual reaction to danger. It is a part of nature's design to protect us and help us survive. However, if we deal with too many stressful stimuli at the same time, and if we are dealing with a constant onslaught of stressors in our lives, it can adversely impact our mental and physical health.

We now understand that our bodies get stressed as a natural defense system against danger and any perceived threats. When we feel stressed, the body gets inundated with hormones; our adrenaline starts pumping, and our system prepares itself to either fight or flee from danger.

We as humans respond to challenges or threats with a partially physical response. Our body has the capability of understanding and assessing the possible threat, and those resources we possess help us decide how to act in a threatening circumstance. We assess the danger, the risk, and its worth, and then proceed accordingly.

Stress is our body's natural response and its way of protecting us from putting ourselves in harm's way.

How Does Science Define Stress?

Scientists hardly ever use the term "stress" as a definition because it is so utterly subjective. There is no singular way to define stress, and therein lies the problem. How can you gauge something you cannot define?

The general definition of stress that you can find in dictionaries is a physical, mental, or emotional strain or form of tension. We use the word "stress" so easily in our everyday language nowadays that it feels like it's always been a part of our vocabulary even though it hasn't. Tracing the origins of the word through the previous centuries, we can for sure say that it has been a part of everyday language since the early 14th century. However, stress as a concept—the way we perceive stress now—is still fairly modern.

Stress was a part of the 14th-century lexicon but was hardly ever used to describe a fraught psychological state. Psychological distress might be implied sometimes but it was more often used to describe adversity, struggles, hardships, misfortunes, and maladies (Kennard, 2008).

The concept of "stress" was constantly evolving with new scientific discoveries. As we entered the 18th and 19th centuries, the world was undergoing a serious period of scientific progress. The Industrial Revolution was in full swing, and science and technology were progressing faster than they ever had before, so the world seemed vast, full of possibility and untapped potential. We were rethinking everything we knew or had previously believed, so our thoughts about stress were also changing.

Language had to keep up with science so that these changes could be accommodated and explained to the public.

Physicists had been using the term "stress" for a long time to define elasticity. Elasticity is the ability of a material to bounce back into shape after being stretched or compressed by outside forces. Hooke's Law of 1658 states that "the magnitude of an external force, or stress, produces a proportional amount of deformation or strain in a malleable metal" (Marksberry, 2011).

Simply put, this definition is talking about malleable metals. Malleable metals are metals that can be molded to change their shape of form. The definition states that if you exert force on a malleable metal, it can change its shape or form as a result of the strain. Expressions like strain, resilience, pressure, and elasticity became more commonplace, traveling over from physics to medicine and psychology. Other expressions used in physics such as breaking point and snapping are still used to define emotions and behavior today (Kennard, 2008).

Many people believe Hans Selye was responsible for adopting the term stress into the field of psychology. That is not entirely correct. Selye did have some important contributions toward understanding the effects of stress on the body, but his discoveries brought about a lot of confusion before things could be sorted out and understood entirely. What Selye did was add to the ideas that were already developing about stress by introducing a three-stage process called the general adaptation syndrome or GAS.

Selye claimed that stress is a comprehensive "response of the body to any demand of change" (Marksberry, 2011). He came to this conclusion after conducting a series of tests on laboratory animals.

He started experimenting with stress after finishing his medical training at the University of Montreal in the 1920s. He embarked on this journey after observing patients at a hospital. He said that every hospital patient looked sick and in distress, regardless of the disease they were suffering from because they were dealing with so much stress.

He hypothesized that stress is a nonspecific strain on the body, which occurs when there are irregularities in our body's normal functions. He believed that these irregularities triggered the release of stress hormones in our bodies (Kennard, 2008).

To prove this, he started conducting his experiments on lab animals. In his experiments, he constantly subjected these animals to a constant stream of annoying stimuli, such as blinding lights, grating sounds, blaring sounds, constant changes in temperature from being extremely hot to extremely cold, and other noxious stimuli. He studied the animals' reactions and discovered that these animals, after being under constant pressure and strain, developed diseases most commonly found in humans and hardly ever in animals in the wild.

The constant exposure to stressful situations caused the animals to start experiencing some serious pathological changes. They developed stomach ulcers, their adrenal glands grew larger, and they experienced shrinking of the lymphoid tissue.

His experiments proved that experiencing constant stress could cause these animals to get sick and even develop diseases that they are not naturally prone to.

The animals started getting heart attacks, their kidneys would fail, or a lot of them were suffering from arthritis. At the time these experiments were being conducted, the scientific community believed that these diseases were caused by specific but various pathogens. They believed there was a separate pathogen responsible for causing each specific disease.

For example, they believed tuberculosis was caused by the pathogen *Tubercle bacillus*; syphilis was caused by a *spirochete*; anthrax was through *Bacillus anthracis*; and so on. Selye's theory was contradictory to this popular belief at the time. He said that these diseases could be caused by exposure to grating stimuli as well as pathogens (Marksberry, 2011).

Selye believed that to respond to an external stressor, we have to respond first by coming into action and utilizing our physical resources to either evade the stressor or deal with it. This stage is called the "alarm stage."

Selye's second stage is the "resistance stage." In this stage, we have to try to cope with the external stressor or adapt to it. Then we would reach the third stage, which is the "exhaustion stage." We become exhausted after we have to deal with the stressor again and again without being able to run away or deal with it.

Selye didn't use the term "stress" to define his findings until 1946. However, his theories went viral at the time and stress became a new word that everybody started using. His theories did garner a lot of attention and eventually took on a life of their own. The media turned the word "stress" into a buzzword but disregarded Selye's original definition entirely. Soon, the word made its way into the everyday lexicon, and people started using it to define anything unpleasant or annoying that they had to deal with.

Stress became an umbrella term for frustration and mental strain. People also started associating stress as the cause for physical discomfort, manifesting through heartburn, headache, chest pain, and palpitations. Some people also referred to stress as the consequence of these symptoms such as stomach ulcers or heart attacks. There was a lot of confusion in the scientific community because nobody could agree upon what exactly is stress; is it a cause or a symptom? The *British Medical Journal* defined stress in 1951 as, "Stress in addition to being itself, was also the cause of itself and the result of itself" (Marksberry, 2011). That probably made things more confusing.

So what exactly is stress now?

Stress is a multifaceted word that we use in several ways and for different intents and purposes. When someone we know claims to be stressed, we understand what they are talking about and generally perceive stress as negative. However, that's not always the case.

Medical professionals say stress is a completely normal reaction everybody experiences and is essential for our survival and development. Our bodies are created to handle stress. When we are faced with challenges or changes, our bodies respond by producing both physical and mental reactions. These reactions are considered to be stress.

This doesn't mean that stress is pleasant or a state that we should strive to achieve. In terms of research, stress encompasses biochemical, psychological, behavioral, and psychological effects (Kennard, 2008).

Is Stress a Mental or Physical Problem?

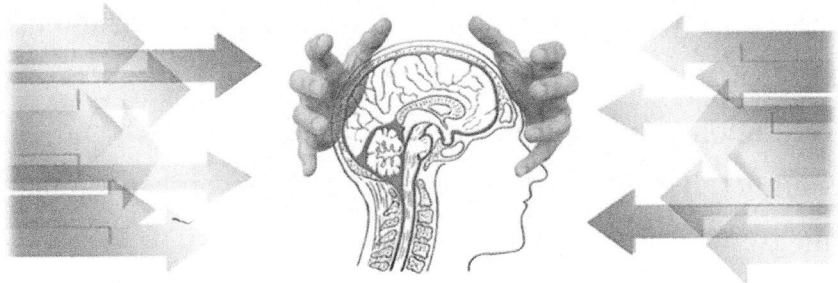

A lot of times, people wonder whether stress is a mental health issue or if it is a physical symptom that occurs due to external factors. Is stress even a mental health issue or is it a normal reaction meant to be experienced by every human being?

Feeling pressure is a major part of being human. As we grow up, the pressure we face in our everyday lives increases. We need to feel pressure to get motivated, to generate energy to complete our tasks, and to accomplish things. However, too much pressure can become detrimental to our mental health, especially when we feel too overwhelmed by our problems and can end up developing stress-related disorders such as anxiety and depression.

In young people, constant pressure and stress can interfere with their developing brains' cognitive function. Being under intense pressure makes it incredibly hard for students to concentrate and can also cause problems in their developing personality, such as creating insecurities, low self-worth, and negative body image.

In adults, pressure can be fatal. A lot of people commit suicide as a dire consequence of not being able to handle the stresses and pressures of day-to-day living. The *British Medical Journal* effectively states, "stress can kill people," and this is 100% accurate (Marksberry, 2011). Stress can and does kill people and is one of the major underlying factors for a lot of mental health issues.

It is imperative to say that stress is not a bad thing entirely. Stress can help your body adjust to unfamiliar situations. It can help keep us alert and positive, wary of our surroundings, and assess risk. It is an essential response in the animal kingdom to keep the animal safe from predators. It works the same for humans, too. For example, the stress of having to perform well at work can motivate you to perform outstandingly, getting a raise and a promotion. Or, if you have a big test coming up, your body's natural stress response can help you stay more alert and awake, enabling your body to work harder than it normally would.

However, stress becomes problematic once it becomes constant and unrelenting. The constant onslaught of stressors without any relaxation or relief can become very detrimental to both our physical and mental health.

Constant mental strain or stress can take a toll on our physical health. Stress can destroy our immune function, really negatively impacting our quality of life. It affects our everyday interactions with other people, how productive we are at work, and how affectionate we are in our relationships.

Michael West, the writer who contributed this article in the *British Medical Journal* claims that we manage to cook ourselves up a toxic stress cocktail, which is a combination of a highly demanding workplace without having a lot of support or control over our lives. We often see this manifesting in single mothers who try to juggle hectic work life with hectic home life, people who work in high-pressure jobs, and caregivers who have to take care of other people around the clock (U.K. Counselling Directory, 2015).

As human beings, we simply must take the time out to decompress. This is essential. We need to find ways to alleviate our stress, otherwise, it could end up being potentially fatal to us. Everybody handles stress differently, with some people more prone to feeling stressed while others are better equipped to handle stress. It has a lot to do with our different personalities, but we can learn how to manage our stress better as well.

Stress can lead to anxiety, which can lead to suffering from full-blown panic disorders. Anxiety caused by stress can develop very early in a person's childhood and consistently impacts us all our lives. There are many different productive and healthy ways that we can adopt that can help us deal with stress (U.K. Counselling Directory, 2015).

Therapy is generally the best option, as a good therapist can help a person who is suffering from stress and anxiety identify the reasons and work toward improving the situation. Therapy can be restorative and give people who suffer from stress and anxiety a second chance at development.

Why Do We Feel Stressed?

We feel stressed when our body has a physical reaction to mental strain and pressure. Whenever we feel threatened or challenged, our body responds by producing stress hormones and chemicals that help us cope with the situation.

When we feel stressed, our bodies produce large amounts of chemicals. The chemical cortisol, also known as the stress chemical, is produced alongside norepinephrine and epinephrine. The production of these chemicals activates certain physical reactions in our bodies.

When our systems are flushed with cortisol and its accompanying chemicals, our blood pressure increases, and our muscles tighten because our muscle preparedness heightens. We end up sweating a lot and become much more alert and aware of our surroundings. Have you ever noticed your hands getting clammy and your heart beating fast whenever you're nervous, scared, or excited? That's the work of these chemicals flooding through your body.

Being alert and aware with heightened senses is beneficial when facing a threatening or dangerous situation. The production of epinephrine and norepinephrine is the reason why our hearts end up beating faster (Felman, 2020).

Any external stimuli that trigger these reactions in our body are called stressors. These can be environmental factors or circumstantial factors. There can be a vast number of stressors in our lives. Some of the most common ones include extremely loud and annoying noises, people acting violent or aggressive, an out-of-control vehicle, and even horror movies or meeting someone you have a crush on. The more stressors you have, the more stressed you end up feeling.

The American Psychological Association conducts a stress survey every year. When they conducted their annual survey in 2018, they discovered that the most common reasons why people feel stressed were because of their jobs or financial issues. Most people get majorly stressed worrying about doing better at their jobs or keeping their jobs and whether they have enough money to survive (Felman, 2020).

Of course, we all have our unique set of stressors as well. Dealing with stress has a lot to do with how we identify these stressors as our triggers and cope with them accordingly. That will be discussed in detail in the upcoming chapters.

Chapter 2:

Stress Triggers, Signs, and Symptoms

In the previous chapter, we discussed all that stress was and the history of the term as we know it today. In this chapter, we will talk about what are the factors that cause us to become stressed in the first place. We know that stress is created due to a physical reaction in our systems, responding to any perceived threat or danger, but what causes us to feel this way? How do we get to the point of feeling threatened or challenged?

Let's discuss the factors.

What Are Stress Triggers?

We all have things that drive us over the edge or take us to our breaking point. We all get triggered by certain situations that adversely affect our mental health and feelings of well-being.

Some people naturally are a bit high-strung and tend to feel stress and pressure more than others. However, that doesn't mean that they are ill-equipped to manage stressful situations; it just means they have a different threshold for stress.

Your stress levels—basically how tolerant you are to stress—is determined by how you respond to the demands of the world. There are a lot of common stressors in the world that have some type of impact on everybody, but we all experience these stressors in our unique ways.

Our personalities have a lot to do with the way we handle stress in our lives. Our genes and life experiences also play a part in determining how we handle stress. We all deal with the constant curveballs life throws at us, but we handle it in our own way. For instance, an upcoming deadline for an important project at work might make some people panic, while others could thrive in such an exhilarating situation because they work well under pressure.

Everyone in the world gets stressed; there isn't a single person on Earth that is completely stress-free. We all have triggers and stimuli that pressurize and frustrate us. We all have reasons why we feel tense. If we want to manage our stress better, we need to figure out what exactly is the source of our stress and how we can eliminate that source or reduce its impact in our lives to help us cope much better.

Stress that is short term or acute is pretty normal and doesn't do us any harm. It can help keep us healthier and more alert.

However, if we keep experiencing stress and it becomes chronic or long term, it can take a toll on our mental and physical health. This is why it is so important to understand your stress triggers—the factors that cause you to stress—so you can do something about this pressure before you implode.

Stress triggers are scientifically called stressors. Stressors are any stimuli that cause you discomfort, frustration, annoyance, or strain. Here are a few common stress triggers that most people experience:

Work-Related Stress

One of the most common types of stress that people experience is work-related stress. Whether you're an adult with a job or a child at school, your duties and responsibilities can be one of the major reasons why you feel so stressed out.

Some of the most common work-related stressors include preparation for exams. Whether you're taking an exam at school as a student or giving a professional exam, the process takes a serious toll on your mind and body. Worrying about whether you would pass or not and the consequences of failing can be very stressful. This kind of stress is usually acute and doesn't last long after the exam is over, so it can help us perform better.

People also get stressed about work deadlines. If you have an upcoming project deadline and have not managed to finish your work on time or if you are scrambling to get your work done last minute, it can be a very stressful experience.

One of the main reasons why people get stressed is worrying about whether they would lose their job. Job insecurity can cause you a lot of stress and is a chronic source of stress. Similarly, if you've been unemployed for a while, it can also be a very stressful situation because you're constantly worried about finances and how you're going to survive. When your survival is threatened, your body goes into its fight-or-flight mode, inundating your system with stress hormones and chemicals, causing you to have a physical and emotional response to this stressor.

Losing your job can make you feel angry, uncertain, afraid, hurt, and depressed. That's normal. You need to take time to process through the upheaval in your life, and it's perfectly fine to feel anxious because you don't know how things will turn out.

Another major fear that people have is the fear of retirement. Retirement is a scary prospect because you are undergoing a very major transitionary period in your life. This can cause a person to become stressed in a number of ways.

First, if you're used to working, the prospect of having a lot of free time all of a sudden might be unnerving. A lot of people are used to being productive and working and also get used to their workplace environment. Losing all of that suddenly can be very stressful. You go from being a lively, productive, contributing member of society to someone who now has nothing to do. You can look for hobbies and interests to pursue, but that realization often comes later.

Another fear that people have associated with retiring is the fear of not being able to make ends meet. If you have not managed to save up a nest egg, or a retirement fund, the prospect of having to provide for yourself in your old age could be a scary one. People get stressed wondering if they would be able to support themselves if they are unable to work, or if they would have the support of their children and family. These are all uncertainties in life that stress people out over.

Change is scary for anyone and can be very stressful as well. If you lose your job, you can end up feeling pretty worthless and lose your sense of purpose in life. It can also negatively impact your self-esteem (Segal, 2017).

Studies have shown that stress at the workplace is one of the top leading causes of stress in adults all around the world. People report feeling stressed about several things at work, from disagreements with colleagues, lack of support by the organization, a high-intensity environment, or a rude boss. Most people who experience work-related stress take it as a part of the job and hardly ever try to seek help or support. However, high-pressure work environments can have some pretty devastating consequences on workers' mental health (Kilburn, 2019).

The correlation between work stress and poor mental health has been extensively documented over the years. In fact, in countries like Japan, which are considered to have some of the most intense work environments, people either die due to stress-related complications or commit suicide. Unfortunately, suicides by disillusioned workers who were unable to cope with the stress in Japan are all too common.

It is so common in fact that the Japanese have a specific term for it. They call it *karojisatsu* which means "overwork suicide." It is a term that everybody knows in Japanese society. Japan puts such emphasis on perfection, work ethic, and productivity that people cannot cope with the stress of having to match such lofty expectations. Their jobs are not only mentally stressful—a lot of them are physically taxing as well.

This means that occupational sudden mortality rates are high. Occupational sudden mortality means when somebody dies because of the pressures at work. The Japanese have a term for this phenomenon as well as it occurs all too frequently. It is called *karoshi*, which means "death by overwork" (Engelmann, 2018).

The death toll of people who committed suicide in Japan due to work-related stress amounted to 1,918 in 2020. The numbers had been steadily rising since 2011, with almost 2,700 victims overall who have taken their own lives (Engelmann, 2018).

Stress at the workplace can impact how well you do your job, so it's like a double-edged sword. Stress about performing well at work can cause you to underperform if the stress is excessive and debilitating. You need to take measures to save yourself from being negatively impacted by constant stress and figure out how you can get more job satisfaction and improve your well-being at your workplace.

This is how you can help manage workplace stress better (Kilburn, 2019):

- **Always Try to Be Organized:** The more organized you are, the less stressed you'll feel. Try to prepare for the new day in advance so that you can save time and work efficiently. Use a planner to create a schedule for yourself, as it will help you stick to it. You can invest in a tangible planner or use a planner app on your phone.

- **Take a Break:** Some people try to power through the day working nonstop without even taking their designated break. The only thing you're doing this way is ensuring that you'll run out of steam pretty quickly. Take advantage of your designated breaks and use that time to decompress. Remove yourself from your workroom, change the scenery, and get some fresh air. You don't have to take a very long break; even a five-minute break can help break the tension and refresh your mind.

- **Don't Try to Do Everything Yourself:** A lot of us are perfectionists and would rather take on more work to ensure everything is done properly than to entrust the task to someone else. Let loose a little and learn to trust your colleagues. Don't hesitate to delegate tasks if you're struggling and overwhelmed by your workload. This gives you more time to focus overall on what is important.

- **Share Your Problems:** A lot of us hesitate before talking to our boss or superior because we don't want to seem demanding or difficult. However, the best way to find solutions without making any wrong decisions is by talking to the boss. Discuss what problems you're facing and get their feedback about how to improve the situation. Your boss will appreciate your initiative.

- **Change Your Job:** If you hate your current job and don't think it has any redeeming qualities, then switch! It seems difficult and it can be, but it will be beneficial for you overall in the long run. We can get stuck in a rut doing the same thing over and over again—not feeling challenged or motivated to do better in the least. If you feel like you're in such a situation at your workplace, quit and find a place that will make you happier. You'll feel free and might also find a job that offers better financial incentives.

Financial Stress

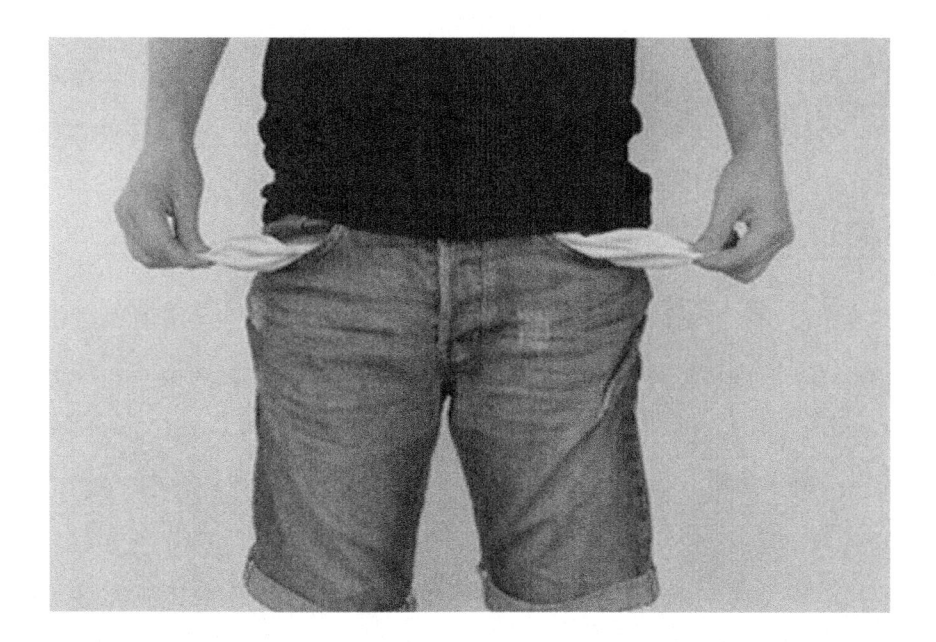

Only a handful of people in this world are exempt from experiencing financial stress. Financial stress is the most common type of stress. Almost everybody experiences some type of financial strain in their lives at some point. For most, finances are a constant source of stress in everyday life.

One of the biggest sources of financial stress is worrying about having enough money to live a comfortable life. A lot of people living paycheck to paycheck suffer from constant stress worrying about how they are going to pay the bills, put food on the table, and still have enough money to deal with everyday expenses (Segal, 2017).

Debt is another cause of financial stress. If you have a large debt to pay off, maybe you have mounting credit card debt, student loans, or a mortgage; you're always worried about making the payments on time. Paying back debt can be a huge deterrent holding you back from having savings or acquiring wealth and property.

Getting unexpected large bills can also cause a lot of financial strain. A lot of us manage our finances by being on a strict monthly budget. If that budget is derailed by an unexpected bill, maybe the car broke down and needed to be repaired; maybe somebody got sick and you got stuck with a large medical bill, or something in the house that needed fixing; life is full of unexpected expenses, and they can be a huge source of financial stress.

Financial stress can be devastating for your relationships and mental health. According to the Fitch Law Firm, financial stress is the leading cause of divorce in American couples (Soilson, 2015).

A study was recently conducted by the Institute of Divorce Financial Analysts, where it was discovered that financial trouble was the third most common reason cited for divorce. It stated that over 22% of all cases they assessed showed financial stress was the main reason for their divorce (Bernstein, 2016).

The most common reason was incompatibility, and often, that incompatibility had a lot to do with disagreements over how to deal with money.

Fitch Law firm claims that financial stress can destroy a relationship, chipping away at the love and affection that the couple feels for each other because the stress consumes everything else in the relationship (Soilson, 2015).

Experiencing this can be devastating because going through such financial strain can exhaust a person emotionally, eating up their resources to the point where they are not able to be in a healthy relationship.

Coping with it can make you feel quite alone and depressed, but you're never alone. These are the most common stress triggers in the world, so everybody has felt what you are feeling at some point.

Here are some ways you can help deal with financial stress:

- **Take On the Challenge:** A lot of people try to escape their financial stress by being in denial and not accepting their current situation—that will only lead to more stress and anxiety. You need to figure out why you're financially stressed, and think about ways to tackle the situation. Crunch the numbers; create a budget and figure out where you can save more money and how you can earn more. Think about solutions instead of feeling sorry for yourself.

- **Create a Budget:** A budget can help you track your finances and manage your money more easily. You should know how much money you make, what sources of income you have versus your monthly expenditures. Stick to that budget to take away the uncertainty of not knowing where your money goes every month. Many great apps help you budget your money. All you have to do is download whichever one you like and enter your details; it's that easy.

- **Get Help:** If you don't have a head for numbers, you can always ask your family or friends to help you. An outside opinion can help analyze your spending and they can give you some useful insight about where you can make cutbacks on your spending, and they might even have ideas on how you can utilize your money better. If you can get the help of someone who knows about finance, that's for the best; you can always go online and educate yourself; or go to the local bank and see what resources they have to offer you for free.

Health-Related Stress

Health is another common stress trigger. A lot of us are health conscious and want to be at optimum health, while some of us are sick and want to get better as soon as possible. There are many reasons why health can be a stress trigger for people.

We could be ill or fear getting ill which can cause stress in our lives. Injuries can be very stressful, as they force us out of our normal lifestyle, and we end up becoming confined and restless for some time.

Being pregnant is also very stressful. Not only is the body going through so many physical changes but your mental health is also affected. Your body changes, you gain weight, and you develop many unpleasant symptoms, and this can be quite jarring, especially for somebody who has never been pregnant before. On top of that, the concern for the baby's health is paramount as well; all in all, this creates a very stressful situation.

If someone in your life has recently passed away, it can be seriously stressful and can take a hard toll on your mental health. There is no comparison to the anguish we feel at the death of a loved one. You know that your loved one will never be in your life again; you would never be able to talk to them, hug them, or spend time with them. It seems like the world will never be a happy place again, and that can take you to a very dark and stressful place.

Dealing with the grief of losing a loved one is one of the most stressful things you would ever experience in life. The stress and pain that you feel from losing your loved one can be quite overwhelming and could make you feel a whole range of weird and difficult emotions that you normally wouldn't experience. You could feel numb, shocked, betrayed, angry, guilty, and profoundly sad. Sometimes the weight of these emotions can feel like it's crushing you (Segal, 2017).

There's no manual on grieving. There's no right way to deal with the loss of a loved one, however, there are healthy coping mechanisms that you can employ to help alleviate your sadness and accept the new normal in your life. It is essential to help you move on.

If you suffer from a mental illness such as anxiety or depression, you'd naturally be more prone to stress. People who suffer from mood disorders also experience a lot of stress, along with people who are on the autism spectrum. They experience stress very differently and can be stressed by a lot of different things that people who are not on the spectrum wouldn't even think twice about.

Suffering from a chronic health problem can also be stressful, especially if you have symptoms that affect your quality of life. Being in pain, feeling sick, and feeling tired can all be very stressful.

The worst part is that stress adds to the sickness your body feels, so it's harder to get better. Stress can take such an immense toll on your body, both physically and mentally, that it often aggravates existing health conditions, making it much harder to recover.

Stress can make you ill. It can weaken your immune system, make you feel tired, make your muscles ache, make you feel depressed and anxious, and cause your stomach to be upset (Kilburn, 2019).

Here are some ways to help combat health-related stress:

- **Work Out:** Regular exercise can help boost your immune system and perk up your mood. It also helps improve your circulation and is good for preventing heart disease. Exercise produces endorphins, which bust stress and make you feel happier. Producing endorphins makes you feel good and can burn off the extra stress hormones in your body.

- **Take a Break:** Sometimes adults need a time-out, too. You should never force yourself to work if you just don't feel up to it. Take a break. Grab a cup of tea or coffee, and sit outside for a bit to breathe. Get help if you need it. If you don't, you'll burn yourself out and ruin your chances at productivity altogether. Taking regular breaks to decompress can help you feel better. Not doing so can make you feel ill!

- **Take Supplements:** Being stressed can drain vital minerals from your body which are so important because they improve our immune system. Minerals like magnesium and zinc are vital for the healthy functioning of our immune system. See what supplements you can take or which foods are rich in zinc and magnesium, and incorporate those into your diet. You will feel much better.

Relationship and Social Stress

Being in a relationship can be very stressful. You need to maneuver through life, keeping not only your feelings and values in mind but your partner's as well. It can be very challenging trying to keep a healthy relationship with your partner. You need to know how much you can give and when you can take or how much to compromise and when to put your foot down.

It's figuring out the correct balance that can be incredibly stressful. It's pretty normal to feel stressed out in a romantic relationship. You could be stressed about keeping your partner happy, you could be stressed worrying about your partner's fidelity, or stressed to maintain a relationship that is hard work.

People usually make the mistake of keeping their stress under wraps. They bottle up their emotions and never share what is on their mind, expecting their partners to be mind readers, driving them up the wall trying to guess their needs and anticipate their moods. This kind of approach makes it hard for partners to figure out what it is they need from each other, creating misunderstandings and an inability to provide the support that is needed.

If you keep brushing stress under the rug and not deal with it, it can get you stuck in a negative cycle where you can actually "catch" your partner's stress. Yes, it's contagious. If we see our partners stressed, we tend to take on their stress. If you've ever had an argument that got the better of the both of you, you might have noticed that even if one person was calm when the argument started, halfway through both ended up being hyped up and frazzled because they caught on to their partner's stress (Shrout, 2018)!

This can make you say the thing you regret, make snide comments that you didn't mean, and overall hurt your partner's feelings which you never intended to do. Couples can get trapped in such a cycle and become too overwhelmed by stress to solve their underlying problems.

There are other types of relationship and social stresses that you can experience as well.

A lot of people feel stressed about public speaking. Some people end up getting so scared that they throw up or run off stage. This is the fight-or-flight response acting up at its peak. People get nervous, they choke, their throat jams, and their hands get clammy.

People also experience stress before a first date or in the initial stages of dating when they want to make a good impression on their partner. A lot of people feel stressed in social situations where they have to interact with strangers or meet people in large groups.

Getting married can be an incredibly stressful time in your life. Not only do you have to plan a wedding, which can be one of the most stressful experiences of your life, you also have to worry about finances, worry about your new partner, and worry about whether you're making the right decision. Marriage is a big step in anybody's life, so there are always some cold feet and second thoughts. The entire experience is very stressful which is why so many things can and do go wrong.

Getting divorced is a different kind of stress. Some people feel quite happy and relieved after getting divorced while others feel devastated and broken. Regardless, it is a time for great emotional upheaval in a person's life and can naturally be very stressful.

Having a baby and raising young children can also be causes of great stress. Taking care of a baby is a lot of work, especially if you're a new mother. You've just given birth, your body is tired and feels broken, and you're constantly caring for the baby and not getting enough sleep. Safe to say, the first year of your baby's life can be the most stressful time for the parents.

Raising your children is also very stressful because your responsibilities change every few years as your children grow up. You go from worrying about bottles and pacifiers to school books and toys and when they become teenagers—that's when the real stress and worrying begins. Parents of teenagers are constantly under duress, especially if their teenage children are rebellious and prone to disobeying and acting out.

Being a caregiver is also one of the most stressful jobs you can have. People often become caregivers for the elderly or infirm relatives or friends. This is a physically and mentally draining job with little reward and a lot of demands. It's also a mainly thankless job, and caregivers often end up feeling dejected, depressed, fatigued, and even suicidal.

We all experience stressful relationships throughout our lives. If we're dealing with other stresses such as work or money, relationship stress can get too overwhelming, which is why most marriages and relationships fall apart. When we carry the stress home with us, we end up single-handedly destroying our relationships because it all gets too much to deal with.

Here are some ways you can help manage relationship stress (Kilburn, 2019):

- **Talk It Out:** Don't be afraid to communicate. If you're feeling stressed out or under pressure, share those feelings with your partner. Don't expect them to read your mind. They won't know how you feel unless you tell them.

- **Don't Be Afraid of Space:** Ask for your space when you feel overwhelmed. Being in a relationship does not mean living like conjoined twins. You need your own space to find your bearings and center yourself. You need to establish your own identity, have your independence, and prioritize your needs. Only then can you take care of another person.

- **Get Counseling:** Therapy can help mend damaged relationships because the unbiased professional guides you and helps you navigate through your challenges. A professional counselor will help you discuss your issues with your partner in a healthy way and help you cope with stress and hurt feelings beneficially.

Emotional Stress

Emotional stress correlates to mental health, and unfortunately, it is something we tend to ignore or minimize because we just don't prioritize mental health as much as we do our physical health.

When a person is diabetic and suffering from a lack of insulin, what do you do? Do you take them to the hospital and get them medication, or do you tell them to ignore it and hope it goes away? Well, if you're a sane person, you'd take them to the hospital and get them help.

Mental illness is just like physical illness, only not as apparent, so why do we ignore mental health issues and hope they take care of themselves? This never helps. It just ends up making us more stressed.

Emotional stress bubbles up out of fear and anxiety. When we're afraid for our safety or well-being or whenever we feel anxious about a certain situation, we are adding more stress to our mind and body.

Other causes of emotional stress include low self-esteem, lack of confidence, and poor body image. If you lack confidence, you'd never feel comfortable asking for help or putting your foot down, so you're likely letting other people walk all over you, which can cause serious stress in your life.

Emotional stress also stems from our need to constantly control everything in our lives. When we try to control everything around us, something is bound to go wrong eventually. And when it does, we take that as a failure and beat ourselves up about it, making us feel more stressed than ever.

People often wonder if there is a difference between stress and anxiety. There is but the two often interconnect and overlap each other. Anxiety is a disorder that is caused by overwhelming stress. When we have anxiety, we're overly stressed, we feel sad and depressed, and we're always in a bad mood. It feels like we're falling deeper and deeper down a hole, and it becomes harder to get out because we keep burying ourselves under these negative thoughts and feelings.

It's awful that just because deteriorating mental health is not as apparent as deteriorating physical health, we often end up ignoring it. People never want to admit they are experiencing mental health issues out of fear of being labeled crazy or dramatic and not being taken seriously.

However, taking care of your mental health is equally if not more important than physical health because poor mental health can cause your physical health to deteriorate. We can take our mental health into our own hands and look after it. We can get treatment and take preventative steps that will not allow our mental health to get worse (Kilburn, 2019).

This can be as easy as taking the time to do something you love for yourself or going to see a therapist get professional help.

Here are some ways to help cope with emotional stress:

- **Be More Active:** Lying in bed inert can make you feel more stressed and depressed. Get up and move around. Go for a walk or a swim. Exercise busts stress chemicals like cortisol. Exercising doesn't mean putting in long hours at the gym. Do what makes you feel good! Do yoga, go for a walk, dance, or go kickboxing. It's about being active and moving your body and not about fitness or losing weight. Find exercises that help improve your mood.

- **Be More Social:** Being alone can make you feel more depressed. Lack of interaction with others and not having a human connection can make you feel isolated, depressed, and out of touch. Even if you're an introvert and feel burnout from social interactions, reach out to one friend or family member and talk to them. It helps improve your mood. It breaks the monotony of your thoughts and gives you a fresh perspective to listen to.

- **Do Something For Yourself:** Make sure you do at least one thing a day that makes you happy. Think about it: What makes you happy? Do you like listening to music? Doing arts and crafts? Gardening? Playing with your cat? Whatever makes you happy, even if it is as simple as taking a bath, do it at least once a day. You owe it to yourself. This will help you feel more positive and create good emotions (Kilburn, 2019).

- **Use Essential Oils:** Essential oils can help you feel calmer and more relaxed. Different essential oils nurture different emotions and states of mind. For example, if you can't sleep and feel too high strung, use a little lavender oil to calm down.

General Stress

If the common stressors mentioned above don't apply to you and you can't figure out why you're feeling stressed, you might just be stressed in general. General stress is stress that doesn't have any reason or obvious trigger. It just means that certain things in your life can stress you out, and you haven't yet figured how to handle that stress. We often feel stressed because of our inability to manage our stressful emotions rather than the parts of our lives that we feel are responsible for making us feel stressed (Kilburn, 2019).

If you're undergoing a transitionary period in your life, feeling stress is natural. That is because change is naturally stressful for many people. Even if the change is good, it can still be stressful because we fear the unknown and the uncertain. This kind of stress doesn't last long; we only feel stressed until we find our bearings and can smoothly settle into the new phase in our lives.

How to Recognize and Deal With Stress Triggers

It can be quite difficult to recognize what a stress trigger is for us, as everybody has different triggers. Here are a few things you can do to identify your stress triggers so you can figure out how to cope with them in the long run.

The first thing that doctors recommend you do is keep a stress diary. It doesn't have to be a literal notebook; a stress diary is anywhere you can document your emotions. It should be easy to access, and you should be able to add to it whenever you feel the need to. The notes app on your phone will suffice.

You should jot down the following things in your stress diary whenever you're feeling stressed (NHS Scotland, 2018):

- Where you were when the stressful episode occurred
- The date and time
- Who you were with
- What things or activities you were doing
- How you felt emotionally at the time
- What your thoughts were in that moment
- What actions you took
- How you were feeling physically
- Give yourself a stress rating (i.e., how stressed you felt on a scale of 1–10).

This diary will help you figure out what your stress triggers are and how you act under duress and pressure. It can also help you figure out better coping mechanisms because you'd be able to see how you acted in a situation that worked out in your favor versus how you acted in a situation that didn't, and use that to establish a behavioral precedent for yourself for the future.

We have now talked about some of the most common causes of stress in our lives and how we can cope with these triggers.

Let's discuss the role stress plays in our lives.

Chapter 3:

The Role of Stress in Our Lives

Our lives are becoming more challenging day in and day out. We're far from the idyllic lifestyle our predecessors probably hoped we would be living in the future. Now we're constantly under pressure, dealing with workdays that last 10–12 hours, constantly hustling to make money, to make our place in the world, and simply to survive and be comfortable.

We all want a well-paying job, a career that challenges and motivates us, our own house, money in the bank, and a secure life. We work very hard to accomplish these things, and the effort can be quite stressful and draining. Running this rat race, we hardly ever get time for ourselves or to spend some quality time with the people we love anymore. We are one of the most depressed, emotionally dissatisfied generations, longing for human connections even though communication has been made so accessible for us. Being this disconnected, despite being connected in every other way, is a cause for great stress.

Nothing in life comes for free, so if we want to accomplish something in our lives, we need to dedicate our time and work hard toward it. We put our noses to the grindstone and do what we need to do to create the lifestyle we aspire to live. This process can drain us because it is so taxing. We need to decompress; we need to relax, and we hardly ever do. Hence, we end up feeling alone, sad, depressed, angry, and yes, stressed.

However, is that the only role stress plays in our lives? That is not the case. Yes, too much stress can be bad for us, but stress in measured amounts is good for us and vital for our survival.

Let's explore the role stress plays in our lives to see how important it is, and how we can experience stress without letting it overwhelm us.

Why Do Living Things Experience Stress?

All animals (including humans) have hormones in our bodies that create stress. Animals experience stress if they are forced to make extreme or extensive behavioral or physiological changes in their environment.

Animals experience stress in three different ways. The first is physical stress which they experience if they are worn out or injured. The second is physiological stress which they experience if they are in an environment with an extreme temperature that is beyond their control, and they lack food and water. The third is behavioral, which is stress caused by unfamiliar surroundings or people.

The triggers that cause animals to get stressed out are also called stressors. Stressors for animals could include predatory animals, loud unfamiliar noises, and lack of food and water. Though many animals can adapt and can survive dealing with one or two stressors for some time, prolonged exposure to numerous stressors can cause long-term suffering, distress, and even death in animals (Humane Slaughter Association, 2019).

If you recall Selye's experiments mentioned in the first chapter, exposed lab animals to noxious stressors that caused them to develop kidney failure, heart disease, and other illnesses most commonly found in humans (Marksberry, 2011).

Stress in animals is beneficial if it's acute, just like humans. Stress can help animals survive in the wild, as it keeps them alert to the presence of predators and helps keep their senses sharp to hunt for food and water.

Just like animals, stress also plays an important role in human lives.

Types of Stress

Stress is our body's way of responding to the challenges the world presents to us. Stressors for humans are triggers in our environment or events in our lives that cause us stress. It could be dealing with someone who we find difficult or being in an unpleasant situation. Everybody responds to stress differently, and our bodies respond differently to different types of stress.

There are two types of stressors: long term and short term.

Acute Stress

Acute stress is short-term stress and can be beneficial for us. It is what triggers the fight-or-flight response in our body. Whenever we are faced with a potential threat or challenge, we trigger the acute stress response in our bodies. We feel it all of a sudden, and we feel it intensely. It can also provide a rush. This is what adrenaline junkies crave when they skydive or ride roller coasters. We can feel acute stress when we're on a first date, giving a job interview, or getting pulled over by the cops.

Feeling acute stress now and then isn't harmful to healthy people. However, a very severe episode of acute stress can be quite devastating. For example, you suddenly find out that you're in serious trouble with the law, or receive the news of the sudden demise of a loved one. It can cause mental health issues such as PTSD (post-traumatic stress disorder) along with physical health issues as well, such as getting migraines, having stomach issues, or even getting a heart attack.

Chronic Stress

Chronic means long term, so chronic stress means being under constant stress for a long time. A mild dose of acute stress can help you out by making you more motivated, active, and energized. However, if the stressors in your life keep adding up and don't seem to alleviate, they can be quite damaging.

You can develop serious health issues such as insomnia, chronic fatigue syndrome, irritable bowel syndrome, and blinding headaches. Chronic stress creeps up at you more subtly than acute stress but is far more devastating. You need to be able to recognize and cope with types of stress to be healthy.

Identify Stressors in Your Life

You need to be able to recognize the various sources of stress in your life and figure out how you can cope with them. One of the ways as mentioned in the previous chapter is keeping a stress diary; another is being more observant and making a mental checklist. Notice your patterns and behaviors and see what works for you in specific situations. You'll see how you have certain stressors that are created circumstantially while others seem to spring up from within you.

You need to decipher the source of each.

External Stressors

External stressors are created circumstantially, based on the events occurring around you. Here are some examples of external stressors:

- **Big Life Changes:** Change can be either positive or negative. Even a positive change can be stressful such as getting married, having a baby that you always wanted, getting promoted at work, or buying your own house. Even though all of these are positive factors that make you happy, it doesn't mean that they are not big changes that can't be stressful. These are some of the most stressful experiences of a person's life. Negative changes include divorce, death, or unemployment, and they come with their own sets of challenges and stresses.

- **Your Environment and Surroundings:** Some people are very sensitive to their surroundings, and loud noises, blaring lights, or extreme darkness can be very stressful. Notice how you react to these stimuli, such as moving from a very bright room to a very dark room or hearing a car alarm or fighting neighbors. Loud sounds and bright lights along with very hot or cold temperatures can be causes for stress as well.

- **Unexpected Events:** An unplanned occurrence can throw a serious wrench in your plans and become a cause of great stress. For example, if you get a sudden uninvited house guest, your salary gets cut at work, or your car breaks down, these unpredictable and unfortunate events can be stressful for anyone.

- **Work and Society:** Work stress and social stress have been discussed extensively in the previous chapter. However, it is worth mentioning again, as they are both major causes of stress.

The only way you can cope with external stressors in your life is by being more resilient. You can build up your resilience by taking care of your health. Eat nutritious food, get enough sleep, and be physically active. This helps boost your immune system which in turn builds up your resiliency, so when you do feel stressed, you're better equipped to handle it.

You can also ask other people to help you out if you're feeling overwhelmed. There is no shame in asking for help; everybody needs a helping hand now and then.

You should also learn how to be assertive; being assertive means being confident in yourself. You should be confident enough to stand up for yourself, your beliefs, and give your own opinion and ideas value. If you have a conviction, you should stand by it and make people take you seriously.

Don't take life too seriously though, and have a sense of humor about things. You know that old saying, laughter is the best medicine? Well, it's true. Laughing helps alleviate stress. You can also try honing your problem-solving skills and learning how to manage time better. Figure out how to use your time most productively and prioritize doing activities that make you feel good. Feel free to say no to things that you don't want to do or make you uncomfortable. This will help prevent you from taking on any added stress.

Internal Stressors

Sometimes we end up creating our stressors. We end up giving birth to new stressors based on thoughts, feelings, and insecurities that spring up inside our brains and make us feel anxious and strained.

One such internal stressor is fear. We go through so much of our lives afraid—afraid of trying new things or meeting new people and afraid to effect any type of change in our lives. We are also held back by our phobias. A phobia is an irrational fear like some people have a phobia of heights or drowning. Similarly, some people can fear speaking in public or flying on an airplane. Fear is a wasted emotion sometimes, as it prevents us from living life to the fullest and creates unnecessary stress in our lives.

A little fear is a good thing, as it prevents us from doing something stupid. However, irrational fear can hold us back a lot.

People also feel stressed when they can't control their surroundings or have no idea what to expect from the future. Not knowing kills them, and they act out or do things they regret out of that stress and fear. You can equate the feeling to waiting for a test result for a medical test. People often say they feel better even after hearing bad news because it is better than the uncertainty of no news at all.

Our beliefs, expectations, attitudes, and opinions can also be a source of stress for us. We might never even consider how our beliefs contribute to shaping our human experience, but actually, these thoughts often end up setting us up to feel stressed. For example, if you place a lot of value on success, you're going to stress yourself out to have the best career or do things perfectly.

We can control our thoughts and to some extent our environment, but should we? Our fears, expectations, and attitudes have been with us for so long that changing them is seriously a herculean effort. We can try though, by reframing our mindset and choosing to be more positive. We can always challenge the negativity in our minds, use more opportunities to relax, and discuss our problems with our friends or a therapist (Kollam, 2021).

All living things experience stress from the smallest microbe to a plant—or animals to us. All stress is not bad as we discussed previously, but how do we know which stress is good and which is bad?

Is All Stress Harmful to Us?

It has been mentioned numerous times in this book that mild acute stress is good for us, but how can we tell the difference? It can be confusing because severe acute stress can be damaging for us and so can chronic stress. How do we know which stress is good and which is bad? Can stress even be good? Yes, it helps us survive, but that doesn't make it "good"—that just makes it useful.

We know quite well that stress not only damages us mentally but can also wreck us physically as well. We know that stress can cause cancer, heart attacks, diabetes, and skin conditions like psoriasis, obesity, anxiety, and depression. So it's only logical that we try to remove as much stress as we can from our lives so that we can be healthy.

However, that's not always the case.

Stress can help us out quite a lot in small doses. It also depends on the type of stress we're experiencing.

Researchers have now found that it is not the stress in itself that's harmful; rather it's people's perception of it. The University of Wisconsin conducted a survey in 2012 about stress and how people believed stress affected their health. They tracked the participants of that survey for eight years to measure the impact of stress in their lives (Kaiser Foundation, 2021).

The study discovered that people were only ever at an increased risk of death if they had a lot of stress in their lives and that they believed this stress would kill them. People who had stress but felt like they could manage it were at minimum risk of death; even lesser than those who didn't have a lot of stress in their lives, to begin with (Kaiser Foundation, 2021).

So what does this mean? Well, pretty much the age-old saying, "mind over matter": If you believe your stress will kill you, chances are it probably will. However, if you believe you can conquer your stress through proper management, you're not at the risk of death at all.

It's a matter of changing your mindset (Kaiser Foundation, 2021).

All stress is not harmful. Stress serves its place in nature; it's how we handle it that determines how bad it is for us. Still, there is still a difference between good stress and bad stress.

Good Stress and Bad Stress

Good stress is called "eustress." Eustress is positive stress. It motivates us and improves our functioning. Bad stress is called "distress." Distress is overwhelming and negative and impairs the way we function (Shafir, 2020).

What Is Eustress?

Eustress is a relatively new term that is being used to describe positive stress. This type of stress helps us out by motivating us to work harder, to perform better, and to help us accomplish our goals even when faced with adversity. Eustress is triggered in the body by the fight-or-flight response, same as distress or bad stress.

However, the difference lies in the fact that when we experience eustress, the energy we produce is proportional to the amount of energy we need in that situation. When we are experiencing distress, we produce extra energy that we cannot use.

The kicker here is that you determine whether you're in distress or eustress. How? This is because the state of eustress or distress depends upon your perception of the stressor and yourself. If you're confident in yourself and you know you can handle the stress trigger you're experiencing, then it is safe to say that you're more likely to experience eustress.

The fact that you can positively assess your stressor can help you channel the energy you produce through the fight-or-flight response in a productive way that can help you figure out a way to solve the problem rather than get defeated by it (Shafir, 2020).

What Is Distress?

The meaning lies in the word. Distress is negative stress that is distressing for you and can cause you to feel stressed out and anxious. People who feel distressed can experience feelings of being overwhelmed, incredibly anxious, and sick to their stomach. They might also feel severe headaches, building tension, lack of sleep, inability to concentrate, and constant irritability.

Constantly experiencing intense stress for a long period is quite toxic for your body and your mind. It can cause a whole host of mental and physical illnesses, and it can impair your natural ability to function.

The main difference between positive and negative stress has to do with how you feel your triggers and how you assess them. Distress occurs when you end up assuming that the stressor is beyond your ability to control or solve or change. A lot of people end up feeling dejected and helpless because they are unable to find an effective solution, and as a result, they just keep worrying and feel worse about themselves.

How Can You Identify Eustress and Distress?

Eustress and distress have their signs that you can look out for so you know the type of stress you're experiencing.

Signs of Eustress:

The following are signs that signal eustress (Shafir, 2020):

- You will have productive energy.
- You will feel more focused.
- You will feel motivated.
- You might feel excited.
- The stressor seems like something you can manage.
- It helps improve your performance.
- It builds up your confidence.
- You expect a good outcome.

Signs of Distress:

The following are signs that signal distress (Shafir, 2020):

- You have a lot of restless energy that you won't know what to do with.
- You lack focus.
- You feel lazy and don't feel like doing anything.
- You feel afraid and concerned.
- You avoid dealing with the problem.

- You feel overwhelmed.

- Your performance gets impaired.

- You feel insecure.

- You know that you won't get a good outcome.

Whether you experience eustress or distress has a lot to do with the situation you're in and the environment around you.

You're more likely to experience eustress in situations where you need to concentrate on changing your emotional state. The stress trigger you're experiencing is not that intense and seems like it would soon pass. You might feel confident that you can overcome the stressor in that possible situation. You feel like you're equipped with all the tools you need and the resources within yourself to tackle this issue the way you want it to, and you also have a good support system that will help you deal with this stressful situation in your life. You know that you can use this stressor as an opportunity to affect positive change in your life, as you have all the tools and skills that you need to implement it. You know exactly what to do to reach a desirable outcome so you do it and manage to conquer the situation.

Whether you experience eustress or distress has a lot to do with the type of person you are as well.

You're much more likely to experience eustress if you're more of a solution-oriented person than one for dwelling on problems. You see a problem, and you work on solving it. You are confident in your abilities and know you have everything that it takes to overcome the stressor in your life. If you're optimistic and are excited about effecting change, you're more likely to do it. This gives you more control over the outcome as well because you assertively take control and believe in yourself. You're resilient, and you adapt quickly to new situations, and you want to do the best job you can at all times. You are knowledgeable and prepare yourself to handle new situations and deal with stress. You can also read into the situation to assess its value and figure out whether it's worth spending your time and effort on. If you believe in self-care and value your worth and are compassionate toward yourself, you're much more likely to experience eustress.

Individuals who are more likely to experience distress are the exact opposite.

They don't have any support from other people, most likely because they never asked for it. They are cripplingly insecure and lack confidence, so they are never able to assertively ask for what they need. Every stressor becomes overwhelming for them, and they give up before they even start to try to deal with the situation.

They have a victim mentality and think of themselves as poor and helpless which is why they lack the conviction to overcome the stressors in their lives. They are so scared of making mistakes and failing that they never end up trying in the first place. They are incredibly self-critical and keep playing negative outcomes in their minds over and over again which discourages them from ever doing anything different. This kind of person is most likely to experience constant distress.

Distress is also situational. People are likely to experience distress in situations where there is an onslaught of recurrent stressors. It could also be if the stress is caused by your inability to meet your basic needs or if you're dealing with a serious health problem. Distress can also spring up from childhood trauma or if there are a lot of unfamiliar aspects involved. Other distressing situations include if many stressors are acting at the same time on the same person, and there is no way to work out a positive outcome of the situation. A distressing situation can also be at high stake, where there could be big losses.

Why Do We Feel Eustress and Distress?

There is no single reason why we feel stressed. Every single person on Earth can probably produce a long list of stressors. There is no doubt that there are many stressful situations and events in our lives. How we interpret these factors determines whether we end up experiencing eustress or end up getting distressed.

Data collected on stress from 2014–2017 cited money as the most common source of stress in Americans. This was followed by work stress, the stress of having an unstable political climate, an uncertain future of the country, and increasing incidents of violent crimes. They also listed excessive exposure to media, stress over physical health and illnesses, loneliness, and relationship disputes along with lack of sleep and bad nutrition as causes for stress (Shafir, 2020).

These stressors are almost always going to be perceived as the source of distress. While some stressors can maybe be perceived as causing eustress, such as work stress which can increase motivation and provide the drive to perform better, most of these are pretty distressing. There's no positive way to perceive economic instability or suffering from long-term health problems.

Eustress is almost always acute, transient, and temporary and is experienced when the person has the power to affect the outcome in their favor.

Typical examples of eustress can include getting promoted at work, hosting a big event, or performing in front of an audience. Other examples of Eustress can include having a baby, getting married, or moving to a new city (Shafir, 2020).

How Do Eustress and Distress Impact Us?

Eustress and distress both can impact us in their own unique yet specific ways. Eustress typically has a positive impact on us. It improves our concentration, makes us feel more alert and focused, gives us productive energy that we can utilize toward our work, and motivates us to do better. Distress, on the other hand, negatively impacts us by making us feel depressed, lethargic, demotivated, irritated, and angry.

Chronic distress that keeps happening to us can spike up the levels of cortisol in our bodies; cortisol is one of the stress hormones in our body. This can create a whole host of illnesses, both physical and mental.

Distress can impair our ability to get a good night's sleep. If you're under distress, you won't be able to fall asleep or have trouble staying asleep even if you do end up passing out from exhaustion.

You could experience bad headaches or stomach cramps. You could have an upset stomach or be constipated. You would also probably notice a change in your appetite. You could go from not having any appetite to constantly eating or going from constantly eating to not eating at all.

Your heart rate can also increase, with a spike in your blood pressure and the rate of respiration increasing, too. You'd have a hard time focusing on anything, and remembering things would become a chore. Concentrating on any task would seem impossible because you'd always feel jittery and on edge, like you've had too much caffeine, and you're tweaking.

You'd always feel drained. You'll have no energy and always feel fatigued and exhausted. You won't be able to control your racing thoughts, and whatever thoughts that enter your mind would be annoying, dark, and intrusive. You'd constantly feel lost and not be able to participate in any activities. You'll constantly feel frustrated and end up snapping at friends and family.

You'll always feel anxious, with clammy hands, your stomach in knots, and shivering. The longer you feel distressed, the more damage you'll do to your body. Experiencing distress for a long period can impair your ability to function normally in life and put you at a much greater risk for developing a serious mental illness like depression or anxiety disorders. You can also try to manage this stress by self-medicating and developing a dangerous habit of substance abuse.

The likelihood of developing a chronic illness such as cancer or heart disease will increase tenfold, and your mortality rate will spike up as well. It's a scary prospect, but luckily, it's one that you can change to your benefit with a little effort (Shafir, 2020).

Ways to Prevent Distress and Promote Eustress

All of these symptoms caused by distress sound pretty scary. However, you shouldn't worry, as there are always steps you can take to prevent feelings of distress and promote experiencing eustress.

How? Here are some tips that can help (Shafir, 2020):

- **Focus on Things You Can Control Over Things You Cannot:** You only experience distress when you believe that you're not capable of coping with the stressor in your life. Don't focus on any aspect of the situation that you know is beyond your control. Even if you can't control anything else, you can always control your response to any situation. This makes you powerful. Take your power and use it. If there are any steps you can take to remove the stressor from your life, do it. If there's nothing, you still can control your response to take solace from that.

- **Make Difficult Situations Meaningful:** It's really hard to try to figure out the meaning of painful and tragic situations because it all often seems senseless. However, finding meaning in bad situations can help you be more resilient, optimistic, and resourceful. It can give you clarity about what is important to you and increase your confidence as well. Finding meaning in a bad situation doesn't mean you have to be grateful for the suffering; you just have to turn the situation to your advantage.

- **Figure Out How You Can Impact the Outcome in Your Favor:** Never make yourself feel helpless. Even if you feel like there's nothing you can do in a certain situation, there is always at least one step you can take to influence the outcome in your favor. Taking action in a stressful situation feels much better than not doing anything at all. Even if your action doesn't work, you can at least say that you did something instead of letting yourself become a victim of the situation.

- **Figure Out the Main Causes of Stress in Your Life:** We feel stressed when we deal with painful, strenuous, or difficult things in life. Why is this happening? Is something missing from your life? Why are you feeling stressed? The cause could be anything: a bad romantic partner, a difficult and demanding job, rowdy kids, or bad habits, for example. When you find the cause of stress in your life, you'll be able to try and find a workable solution.

- **Be Kind to Yourself:** We often prioritize being kind to other people, which is good, but we forget to be kind to ourselves. We're always our own harshest critic; blaming ourselves for all of our mistakes and things we did in the past and setting unrealistic goals for ourselves. This is just setting yourself up to fail. If you're kind to yourself, you recognize your self-worth and can motivate yourself to accomplish bigger and better things. People who love themselves allow themselves to make mistakes, learn from them, and then get back up stronger than ever. This can help you get better outcomes in stressful situations.

When Should We Seek Help?

If the stress in your life becomes overwhelming, please do not hesitate to seek help from a professional counselor or therapist. This can improve your quality of life.

You should seek professional help if you're experiencing the following feelings (Shafir, 2020):

- Overwhelming feelings of anxiety and stress that have lasted for more than two weeks

- Not being able to eat or sleep to the point where you feel sick

- Not being able to focus on anything and not being able to concentrate or function because you're so stressed out

- Feeling checked out from reality

- Feeling perpetually zoned out and hazy

- Feeling overwhelmingly sad, tired, and unmotivated to the point where you don't feel like doing anything

- Recurrent thoughts of death, wanting to die, and contemplating suicide

- Abusing drugs and alcohol or self-harming

- Indulging in any bad habits to deal with the stress

Stress has a part to play in all our lives. It is you who decides the extent you let stress govern your life. We can take control of the stress in our lives and make it positive. We know stress is not going anywhere, so we might as well change our perception and make it work for us, rather than suffering from it helplessly.

We now know about the role of stress in our lives. Does stress have an impact on our bodies?

Chapter 4:

The Physical Manifestation of Stress

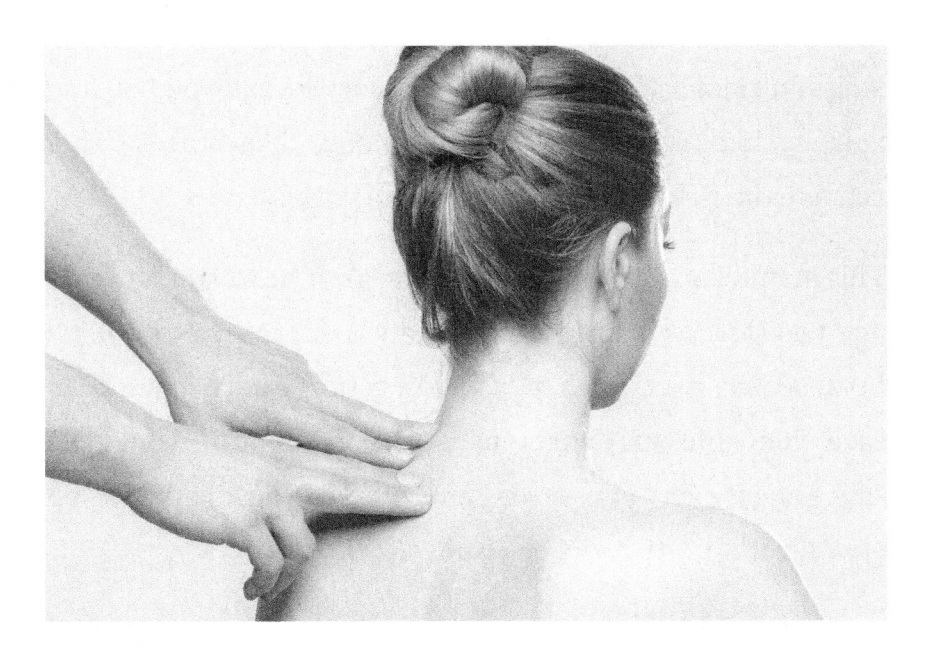

Have you ever noticed that whenever you're feeling particularly tired or upset, it shows on your face? Your eyes can seem puffy and red, you might develop dark circles or under-eye bags, and you might look pale and worn out. That is because mental strain takes a physical toll on our bodies.

Picture this: You're stuck in traffic over 20 minutes late for a meeting that your boss said you absolutely cannot afford to miss. You can feel the stress kicking in; your body tenses up, your muscles start to ache, and your stomach is in knots. You can feel the beads of sweat breaking out on your forehead.

Why is your body doing that?

Well, it's because your brain decided that it's time for you to enter stress mode. The control tower of your brain, which is the hypothalamus, sends out its order. It says, "Release the stress hormones!" It's like an imaginary lever is pulled, and your system is flushed with hormones like cortisol that activate the fight-or-flight response in your body.

This manifests in physical symptoms. Your heart starts to race and you start breathing more rapidly. Your muscles tense up because they're getting ready to take action. This response can save your life in dangerous situations, but if you keep triggering it every day, several times a day, you could mess up your health pretty badly (Pietrangelo, 2017).

How can nervousness or tension or stress ruin our physical health? There is a deeper connection between our mind and our body and this book will explain that connection.

How Does Stress Impact the Body?

Can you believe that stress can affect every system currently inside your body? If you've studied basic biology in school, you would know that our body is a well-connected network of different systems that keep us functional. The respiratory system controls our breathing, the cardiovascular system controls the heart and blood, and our skeletal system holds up the body.

Stress can wreak havoc on all of these systems inside our body including but not limited to the endocrine system, the cardiovascular system, the musculoskeletal system, the gastrointestinal system, the reproductive system, and the nervous and respiratory system. Each system is uniquely yet adversely affected by chronic stress.

How Stress Affects the Musculoskeletal System

When our body is flooded with stress hormones, they cause our muscles to start tensing up. This is almost a reflex reaction because our muscles tense up to protect our body from getting hurt and feeling a lot of pain. When stress suddenly enters our body, all of our muscles become tense at the same time and only let go of the tension once the stress is gone.

If an individual is constantly stressed, their muscles are always going to be tense, in a state of perpetual alertness.

When your muscles are tense for very long, it can start other negative reactions in our body and instigate stress disorders.

Stress can start a domino effect of ailments that can ruin our health. For example, if your muscles are always tense, you could be more susceptible to developing migraine headaches or headaches that you get from tension. This is because you can get a headache if the muscles in the neck, shoulder, and head are chronically tense. You can also experience severe back pain because the muscles in your upper and lower extremities are always tense. This is more prevalent in individuals who experience work-related stress.

If you're someone who is naturally afraid of pain and getting hurt again or if you've only been looking for a physical diagnosis and cure, your recovery might not be as smooth as someone who has maintained some level of activity under the supervision of their doctor. In a nutshell, if you become a vegetable after getting injured or too scared to move because you're afraid you'll hurt yourself again, you're putting more strain on yourself and increasing your likelihood of getting hurt again and having a difficult recovery.

Muscle tension can cause your muscles to atrophy. This means if your muscles remain tense for a long time, they can become useless. If you don't use your body, you're promoting chronic musculoskeletal conditions caused by stress. Not using your muscles can cause them to atrophy, meaning you'd never be able to use them again.

Doctors advise stress-relieving activities for patients who suffer from chronic pain conditions because they have been proven to improve their day-to-day functionality and mood remarkably. (American Psychological Association, 2021)

How Stress Impacts the Respiratory System

Our respiratory system has one main job: to provide oxygen to cells and to eliminate carbon dioxide as a waste product from our bodies. We breathe air in from our nose which goes through the larynx which is inside the throat. From there, air makes its way down the trachea and enters the lungs through the bronchi. Then it is the job of the bronchioles to supply oxygen to our red blood cells, which circulate our body.

When we feel stressed or experience any kind of overpowering emotions, they can manifest as respiratory symptoms in the body. We can feel shortness of breath and can also end up rapidly breathing because the airway present between the nose and lungs becomes smaller.

This isn't a big deal for a healthy person because the body can cope with the extra effort it takes to breathe normally. However, if you're already suffering from respiratory disease like asthma or bronchitis, stressful situations and thoughts can hype up your symptoms and make breathing a serious chore.

Stress can make your breathing rapid, which can cause you to hyperventilate. Hyperventilation can lead to panic attacks; experiencing them is a scary experience for anyone.

You can cope with stress by going to a therapist or a psychologist who will help you work on your breathing by introducing deep breathing and relaxation techniques. They can also implement some cognitive-behavioral strategies so that you can deal with stressful situations better (American Psychological Association, 2021).

How Stress Impacts the Cardiovascular System

The cardiovascular system consists of your heart and your blood vessels. Both these elements collaborate to nourish all the organs in your body and to provide them with oxygen.

Stress can have a direct impact on the cardiovascular system because the stress response triggers activity in this area.

When you experience acute stress, your heart rate can spike up, which means that your heart muscle will be compelled to contract with more strength. The stress hormones in your body such as cortisol, adrenaline, and noradrenaline act as messengers. Your system gets flooded with these hormones, sending a message to your heart that it needs to beat faster.

Have you ever noticed how your heart beats faster after slamming on the brakes in your car to avoid an accident? That's your cardiovascular response to acute stress.

The cardiovascular system also comprises blood vessels that have their response when stressed. The blood vessels have the task of directing blood to large muscles. Stress can cause the heart to dilate, which means the blood vessels have to work overtime to pump blood to these large muscles which causes a spike in your blood pressure. The body calms down once you calm down; once the stressor is gone, your body relaxes.

If you're constantly dealing with chronic stress, it can mess up your heart and blood vessels. The constant rise in heart rate, consistently high blood pressure, and the high concentrations of stress hormones can wreak havoc on your body. This can put you at an increased risk for heart attacks, hypertension, or strokes.

Women and men take on stress differently, so the risk for heart disease caused by stress in women is different as well. The factors change after a woman hits menopause. Before menopause, women have higher levels of estrogen in their body which helps their blood vessels cope better under stress, which makes their bodies more capable of handling stress. This offers them extra protection against heart disease.

However, once menopause begins, the body isn't producing as much estrogen which increases the risk of heart disease in these women (American Psychological Association, 2021).

How Stress Impacts the Gastrointestinal System

A lot of people know that stress can cause stomach problems. However, not many people are aware of how intensely stress damages your gastrointestinal system.

Our gut is designed to function autonomously as it has over a million neurons that are always in touch with the brain. This is why when we feel nervous, we get "butterflies" in our stomachs. Our gut and our brain are pretty close friends. This is why whenever we feel stressed, our gut gets impacted, and we can get a stomachache or experience bloating and other stomach problems.

Scientists have discovered that changes in gut bacteria can cause stress and influence our mood. This shows a strong synergy between the gut and the brain.

Taking on a lot of stress early in life can actually change the way our nervous system develops and how our body responds to the stress it takes on. These changes can actually increase the risk of a dysfunctional gut in later life to a considerable degree.

Stress has a specific impact on different parts of our gastrointestinal system. This is how stress affects various parts of our gastrointestinal system (American Psychological Association, 2021):

- **Esophagus:** Whenever we're stressed, we often tend to have bad eating habits. We might eat a lot or not eat at all. We also tend to misuse alcohol, tobacco, and drugs. This can cause serious heartburn or acid reflux. It can also increase the intensity and frequency of heartburn. Stress can cause the esophagus to spasm, which can feel so intense that we often mistake it for a heart attack. When we're stressed, simply swallowing food can seem more difficult which can cause bloating, gassiness, or increased burping.

- **Stomach:** When we're stressed, oftentimes, we can feel it in the stomach. We might get a stomachache, feel nauseous, or just feel bloated. We might also experience other types of stomach discomfort. Some people even vomit under severe stress. It can also cause a change in appetite. You can get stressed even if you have a bad diet. A bad diet can cause you to be in a bad mood more frequently. People wrongly believe that stress causes stomach ulcers and makes the stomach more acidic. Stress can exacerbate these things, but they are caused by bacterial infections.

- **Bowels:** Most people can feel the change in their bowels after experiencing stress. Stress can cause severe pain in your bowels, bloating, and general discomfort. This is because stress impacts the speed at which food is transported through your body. As a result, you might get constipated or get diarrhea. Stress can also cause serious muscle spasms in your bowels which hurt a lot. It also impacts digestion and determines which nutrients your intestines can absorb. This can also cause a higher production of gas.

How Stress Impacts the Nervous System

The nervous system is the command center of our brain. The nervous system is separated into various divisions. The central division includes the brain and spinal cord along with the peripheral division which includes the autonomic and somatic nervous systems.

The autonomic nervous system is mainly responsible for reacting to stress and branches out into the sympathetic nervous system called the SNS and the parasympathetic nervous system or PNS.

Whenever we feel stressed out, the SNS has a part to play in the fight-or-flight response. Our body dedicates all of its energy sources to the fight-or-flight response.

The whole process starts when the SNS sends a signal to the adrenal glands to release the stress hormones, which are adrenaline, epinephrine, and cortisol. These hormones work in unison with the autonomic nerves which can make our heart beat faster and cause us to breathe rapidly. It also makes the blood vessels in our arms and legs dilating. It can negatively impact our digestive system and our glucose levels so that we are better equipped to handle stress. Long term, this wears out the body pretty quickly (American Psychological Association, 2021).

How Stress Impacts the Endocrine System

When we get stressed, our body responds to the feeling of threat and perceived danger. When our body thinks that we are in such a situation where we might need to either fight for our lives or flee, the brain triggers a domino effect inside our body, which involves the hypothalamic-pituitary-adrenal axis, also known as the HPA. This part of our body acts like a control system, driving the endocrine stress response in our body. When this response kicks in, we produce some pretty serious stress hormones. These include steroid hormones called glucocorticoids, which have cortisol in them.

When we feel stressed, the control tower of our brain—the hypothalamus, which is made of an entire host of nuclei that connect the brain to the endocrine system—sends a signal to the pituitary gland ordering to inform the adrenal glands to amp up the level of cortisol production.

Cortisol does this duty by raising the level of energy fuel we have in our system. It activates the glucose in our body and the fatty acids in our level, kicking them into action. The human body produces varying levels of cortisol throughout the day. We produce the most cortisol when we first wake up in the morning and it gets less throughout the day. This ensures we have a regular energy cycle that helps us make it through the day.

If we are undergoing a very stressful experience, the cortisol levels in our body go through the roof because we need the cortisol boost to deal with the extreme challenge we have to face.

A properly functioning endocrine system is important for keeping us healthy and keeping the effects of stress manageable.

Glucocorticoids are not harmful for us in moderation. Even though they contain cortisol, cortisol in itself is not bad. They actually help keep our immune system healthy and reduce any inflammation in our body. This is extremely important especially because if we are undergoing a stressful or dangerous experience where if we get injured, our immune system comes into play.

However, exposure to chronic stress for a long time can actually sever or damage the communication between the HPA axis and our immune system.

This disrupted communication can be connected to a whole host of physical and mental ailments. These include metabolic disorders like obesity, diabetes, immune disorders, depression, and chronic fatigue syndrome.

How Stress Impacts the Reproductive System

Stress has a different impact on the male and female reproductive systems.

Impact of Stress on the Male Reproductive System

The reproductive system in men is connected directly to the nervous system. The PNS part of the system is responsible for causing relaxation whereas the SNS part causes arousal.

When the fight-or-flight response is triggered in males, their bodies produce testosterone which activates the SNS part of their nervous system—this causes them to get aroused. Cortisol is produced by the adrenal glands, which is important to regulate blood pressure and to enable the regular functioning of the cardiovascular system, circulatory system, and reproductive system. Too much stress can impact the normal functioning of the male reproductive system.

Being exposed to constant stress over a long time impacts how much testosterone is produced in the body. This can cause a serious decline in a person's sex drive and can also cause impotency and erectile dysfunction.

This type of stress can also cause reproductive damage because it reduces your sperm count and can prevent the sperm from maturing. Scientists have discovered that men who live stressful lives have slower sperm, and their sperm can be smaller as compared to men who live relatively stress-free lives (American Psychological Association, 2021).

Stress can also weaken the immune system which can cause reproductive diseases in men, such as infections in the prostate, testicles, and urethra (American Psychological Association, 2021).

Impact of Stress on the Female Reproductive System

Stress can mess up a woman's reproductive system, especially their menstrual cycle. Women and adolescent girls who experience regular stress can experience more painful periods, and the length of their cycle changes. Some might stop having periods for some time altogether and would have an irregular menstrual cycle.

Women experience stress from a lot of different avenues in their lives. Most women have to find a balance between their personal and professional life—juggling family, work, and a lot of other demanding factors in their life. It is unfortunately very common for women to feel stressed, fatigued, or worn out. This can reduce sexual desire drastically.

Stress can adversely impact a woman's reproductive health. Women who are stressed out have a much harder time getting pregnant. Even if they do manage to conceive, stressed-out women have difficult pregnancies and can often experience postpartum depression and other problems adjusting after giving birth. Postpartum depression is intense and very hard to cope with and it can get triggered by excessive stress.

A stressed-out mother can also adversely affect her baby's development. Stress in pregnant mothers can harm the fetus, and stressed-out mothers have a hard time bonding with their new baby after giving birth (American Psychological Association, 2021)

Stress can also result in painful periods and terrible PMS. They can experience cramping, bloating, fluid retention, feeling down, and mood swings.

Women need to especially avoid excessive stress during menopause. As female bodies enter the menopause phase, their hormone levels fluctuate drastically. They end up feeling overly anxious, experience intense mood swings, and generally feel unwell and distressed. Just going through menopause can be a stressful experience not only because it is a transitionary period in a woman's life where she might feel less desirable or could feel old, but she is also likely to experience unpleasant physical changes such as hot flashes which make it hard to deal with.

Women who experience high levels of chronic stress are more susceptible to reproductive diseases. They can get the herpes simplex virus or develop polycystic ovary syndrome (PCOS). They can also develop reproductive cancers as a result of too much stress (American Psychological Association, 2021).

There are also physically evident ways that stress manifests in the body.

Visible Symptoms of Stress on the Body

You can see symptoms of stress appear on the body after experiencing chronic stressful triggers for some time. These include but are not limited to the following:

- **Acne:** Acne is one of the most visible manifestations of stress. This is because acne is clearly visible and most commonly appears on the face. People who are stressed out often have a habit of touching their faces. This can make them break out as it spreads bacteria. There have been several studies conducted to confirm the connection of acne with stress. People often break out during the most stressful times in their lives such as having exams or getting married (Link, 2018).

- **Losing Hair:** Stress can cause your hair to fall out. Stress-induced hair loss is called alopecia areata. This happens when you have immense stress in your life. It can cause your hair to fall out in clumps in weeks and in different patches on your head. It can also cause your entire scalp to become hairless and can also cause your body hair to fall out. It happens because stress causes white blood cells to attack the hair follicles. Another type of similar issue caused by stress is called telogen effluvium. This is a common hair loss problem that is less severe than alopecia areata. It can cause your hair to stop growing and start falling up to three months after a stressful event. However, after the stress has passed, the hair starts to grow again (Scott, 2020).

- **Skin Problems:** Stress can create a lot of skin problems apart from acne. Stress produces excessive oil on your skin which makes it a breeding ground for bacteria which can cause infections, blackheads, and clogged pores. Stress also adversely affects the barrier function of the skin, which causes water loss. This impairs the skin's natural ability to heal itself after getting injured. Stressed-out skin also loses its elasticity over time. You can develop skin conditions like psoriasis, and if you're already suffering from a condition like eczema or psoriasis, stress can make their symptoms much worse (American Academy of Dermatology, 2019).

- **Brittle Nails:** Stress can even manifest itself through your nails. Stress temporarily stops or impairs the production of new nails on a few of your fingers, or it can also be on all your fingers. This might not be evident immediately after the stressful event occurs but can be seen in the weeks following the incident. Certain visible cues show signs of stress on your nails. These include:

  ○ **Beau's Lines:** These are horizontal lines that you can see appear across your nail plate. We all have spotted white dots on our nails. They can appear if we slightly bruise or injure the nail bed and are completely normal. However, Beau's lines are not normal and appear because of stress. These lines serve as literal markers to show where your nail growth has been impaired or stopped as a result of stress. They can occur as a result of both mental and physical stress on the body.

  ○ **Habit-Tic Nail Deformity:** When we feel stressed out, we often tend to pick at the cuticle of our finger or rub our fingers chronically. This can cause trauma to our nails and can cause our nails to grow in an abnormal, dystrophic way. It manifests as a vertical-ridged groove on our nail, which looks a little like a Christmas tree pattern in the center of the nail which starts at the cuticle and ends at the tip of the nail. Stress and anxiety are the main causes of this.

○ **Nail Biting:** Nail biting is a compulsive behavior that is often a result of stress and anxiety. People bite their nails when they feel nervous, anxious, and stressed out. It is a repetitive, compulsive action that is a symptom of a pretty deep-rooted stress-related issue. Many people bite their nails as an emotional release. It helps people feel relaxed. However, it severely damages our nail plate and can cause our nails to separate from the nail bed. This greatly increases the risk of infection and can cause our nails to become sore (Carlos, 2019).

These are some of the most common ways that stress impacts our bodies. We need to take care of our mental health because our physical health and mental health are so deeply connected. When one suffers, it takes the other down with it. Extensive stress can be seriously debilitating. You should always look at ways you can reduce stress from your lives, so you don't end up falling sick as a result of being overly stressed.

How do we do that?

Let's discuss how you can recharge your batteries after feeling worn down by stress.

Chapter 5:

Exhaustion, Burnout, and Fatigue—How to Recharge Your Batteries

Have you ever had days when the world just seems too much

to cope with? When all of your responsibilities seem to tower over you, without any signs of letting up? When you're craving a break and don't feel like doing anything? When all you want is to curl up in a ball in your bed and forget that the world around you exists?

We've all been there. Chances are that if you're feeling this way, you're probably experiencing burnout.

What Is Burnout?

We often use the phrase "burnout" to describe feeling exhausted and when we're just fed up with everything around us. Burnout is a scientifically recognized phenomenon. It is defined as a state of physical, mental, and emotional exhaustion and is caused by prolonged chronic stress.

When you're experiencing burnout, every little thing seems like a big deal, and you end up feeling very overwhelmed by the world around you. You feel like everybody is always demanding things from you, and you're depleted with nothing left to give. You feel completely drained, and you just want to give up because you're not capable of meeting up with the seemingly never-ending demands in your life. As the stress piles up, you lose any drive and motivation you ever had to get the job done and get through the day.

When you're feeling burnout, you can't accomplish anything. Your productivity goes down the drain, and you're running on empty with no energy. You end up feeling completely helpless and lose all hope. You don't believe things will ever improve and end up becoming cynical and feeling resentful as a result. You end up feeling like you have nothing left to offer the world.

When you feel burnout, every area of your life suffers. You can't take care of your home the way you would like, your work suffers immensely, and you have no social life. It can also create problems in your relationships because your cup is so full, you don't have any room to provide support to your partner.

You can get physically sick from burnout. This is because experiencing burnout can create long-term changes in your body and makes you more susceptible to getting colds and flu more frequently. You need to make sure you do everything you can to heal from burnout otherwise you can end up getting sick.

Here's a quick mental checklist you can perform to see if you're experiencing burnout (HelpGuide, 2018):

- Is every day a bad day for you?

- Are you fed up with your work or home life?

- Are you always feeling tired to the point of exhaustion?

- Do you feel like your life is excruciatingly dull, boring, or overwhelming?

- You feel like it's hard to care about anything in your life.

- You feel completely underappreciated or that nothing you ever do makes a difference.

If you ended up answering yes to any of these questions, you're likely experiencing burnout.

How to Identify Burnout: Signs and Symptoms

We all feel terrible sometimes. We have days when nothing feels good, and we feel like everything is too overwhelming; nothing you do ever makes a difference to anyone. You end up feeling helpless, and you're not excited about anything in life. Even getting out of bed seems like a huge task. If you regularly feel like this, you're probably experiencing burnout.

Burnout doesn't happen all of a sudden. It gradually builds up over time, but it can make itself evident to you in that period. The signs might not be that obvious in the beginning, but they definitely get worse and make themselves apparent eventually. This can lead to a mental breakdown if you don't address the situation in time.

Burnout manifests in physical, emotional, and behavioral symptoms.

Physical Symptoms of Burnout

Your body bears the brunt of burnout; it takes a toll on you physically. One of the most common signs of a physical burnout is feeling exhausted all the time. You feel like you have no energy; you're drained and don't feel like doing anything.

You also experience severe headaches because of muscle tension. You can also experience serious muscle pain. If your legs, back, and neck are always hurting for no evident reason, it could be burnout caused by stress.

Burnout can seriously impair your immune system. This means that you are more prone to getting sick because your body is so weak and strained. Burnout can also mess up your sleep pattern. You can either get insomnia and not be able to sleep at all or sleep excessively and don't feel like waking up at all.

Your appetite is also impacted. You either don't feel hungry at all or you're constantly eating from the stress (HelpGuide, 2018).

Emotional Symptoms of Burnout

There are a lot of times that burnout makes itself apparent through emotional symptoms. There's nothing worse than being in a depressed state of mind and feeling completely listless.

When you are experiencing burnout, you can feel completely unsure. You can feel like a failure as if nothing you do in life is successful or worth appreciation. You're always doubting yourself and second-guessing your actions and decisions. You don't have the motivation to even accomplish the simplest of tasks like taking a shower or brushing your hair.

You can feel like you're trapped in your life, and you're stuck in a rut with no progress. You feel completely defeated and helpless. You don't know where you can even begin to make the situation better. Your approach toward life becomes incredibly negative; you turn cynical and look at everything in life with distrust and apprehension.

You feel like nobody is there for you; you feel completely alone and detached from your environment. You don't talk about your problems with anyone because you feel like nobody cares about you. You feel like you're never going to make anything out of yourself in life and nothing ever makes you happy. Some days, you even forget what it's like to smile (HelpGuide, 2018).

Behavioral Symptoms of Burnout

Behavior changes can indicate burnout and are also symptoms of burnout as well. You use the limited resources at your disposal to try and manage your situation, but your coping mechanisms aren't the healthiest. You could end up abusing drugs and alcohol or indulge in harmful behaviors.

You don't feel like doing anything and try to avoid your responsibilities. You withdraw from society and don't interact with anyone. You like being isolated because the prospect of being social drains you. You can also end up overeating which can result in weight gain, which also adversely impacts your body image, making you sad. Similarly, some people can lose a lot of weight as well because they hardly eat.

You can also end up becoming irritable and angry by snapping at others and venting your frustration inappropriately on people who don't deserve it. You can start to fall behind at work or on your chores. You procrastinate because you just don't feel like getting anything done.

You find that you're skipping work more often or you're always tardy. Even when you make it to work on time, you don't feel like doing anything. Your productivity is at an all-time low and you can't even bring yourself to care.

People often use the term burnout with stress interchangeably. While stress is the leading cause of burnout, there is a difference between the two terms (HelpGuide, 2018).

What's the Difference Between Stress and Burnout?

People often confuse stress and burnout. There is a pretty simple difference between the two terms.

Burnout is a consequence of experiencing chronic stress. However, experiencing burnout is not the same as being under a lot of stress. When you're experiencing chronic stress, it means that you're under a lot of strain, and the pressures in your life are too much for you to cope with physically or mentally. However, there are a lot of people who are under stress but believe that they can deal with it or overcome that stress. They know that the stressors in their life will eventually end, and they will feel better again.

However, when you feel burnout, it means that you're not experiencing the typical stress signal that triggers the fight-or-flight response in your body, which kicks you into gear and compels you to take action. People who experience burnout feel completely unmotivated. They don't care about anything; they feel completely fatigued and have given up on life.

If you have burnout, you feel completely hopeless. You don't feel like your life can improve for any reason. Being under a lot of stress can make you feel like you're being suffocated by your responsibilities. However, when you feel this burnout, you feel more like everything in your life is banal and bland. Also, when you're stressed, you know it. With burnout, you don't notice it immediately—it tends to creep up on you (HelpGuide, 2018).

Here are some major differences between stress and burnout (HelpGuide, 2018):

Stress: When you're stressed, you tend to feel like you're spread too thin. You feel like you're involved too much with everything in your life. You tend to have very intense emotions, and you overreact to things a lot. Everything seems very urgent, and you have to get it done immediately. You feel hyperactive, and you feel the intense need to get everything done in a short period.

You feel like you have restless energy and feel anxious a lot. You feel sick, you get headaches, your stomach is upset frequently, and you constantly feel body pain. The damage you do to your body due to stress can cause long-term physical complications and can kill you prematurely.

Burnout: When you're experiencing burnout, you feel completely disconnected from the world around you. You feel utterly dejected. You have no hope and you feel completely useless and helpless. You become very depressed and detached from your environment. You mainly damage your mental health. This can lead to physical complications, but it's your mental health that suffers. You can get suicidal thoughts because you don't see any point in living life. You place no value in your life.

Why Do We Feel Burnout?

A lot of burnout is occupational and happens because of trouble at work. However, anyone who feels overworked and underappreciated can feel burnout. You can be a workaholic office worker who doesn't take designated breaks and hasn't taken a vacation in five years to a single mom trying to juggle work and children at the same time. Caregivers also experience burnout more frequently than other people.

Contrary to popular belief, you don't get burnout just by having a stressful job alone or having to deal with a lot of responsibilities. Various elements can cause burnout, and your lifestyle and personality also has an impact on whether you feel it overall. Your hobbies and interests can also play a huge part in causing excessive stress as a difficult job. All of these factors can contribute to burnout (HelpGuide, 2018).

What Are the Signs of Occupational Burnout?

There are various causes of occupational burnout. Occupational burnout means experiencing burnout because of work-related stress. You feel like you have no control over your work. You feel helpless and stuck in your job. You feel like you never get recognized for your efforts at work or praised or appreciated if you do anything well. Sometimes, you feel completely ignored or neglected.

You feel like your job is too demanding for you, and your boss has unreasonable expectations from you. You could also feel like your role at your job is not clearly defined, so you always feel lost. You could also feel like your job is immensely dull and monotonous; it doesn't challenge you in any particular way.

You can also feel overwhelmed because your work environment could be too chaotic for you. You might not be able to cope with a very high-pressure environment (HelpGuide, 2018).

What Are Lifestyle Causes of Burnout?

Sometimes, we can get burnout because of the way we live our life. We could work way too much without taking any time to unwind or relax. We work because we need to. Some people work two or more jobs to make ends meet. A lot of us are also responsible for juggling home life with our work life.

This kind of intense lifestyle can cause you to have burnout. If you don't have good, supportive relationships in your life, you don't have a healthy outlet for your frustration and stress. This can cause burnout more quickly.

You can also get burnout if you take on more responsibility than you can handle. If you take on more tasks than you can manage without getting any help, you're more likely to experience burnout.

If you're living a high-paced lifestyle where you don't get enough sleep, you're probably going to feel burnout much faster than if you get a good eight hours of sleep every single night. You need to be able to ask for help when you need it, otherwise, you can get overwhelmed very easily.

A stressful lifestyle can also cause emotional distress. It's all like a domino effect. When one thing goes wrong, others tend to go south pretty quickly as well (HelpGuide, 2018).

Which Personality Traits Can Cause Burnout?

Some people are just naturally prone to getting burnout. People who are more prone to getting burnout are those who are perfectionists. If you're always worried about doing things perfectly and you don't feel like anything is ever good enough, you could wear yourself out and get burnout.

People who are very pessimistic and have a negative outlook on life are also more prone to burnout. Pessimistic people always believe the world is always out to get them, and that is a very stressful outlook on life.

Very high-strung people who have Type A personalities are also prone to burnout. These are people who run on a schedule, have multiple to-do lists, and get very upset if they have to deviate from their schedule. They are control freaks and always want to do everything themselves. They don't trust other people and live by the saying, "If you want something done right, you have to do it yourself."

If your personality is like this, then you are naturally more inclined toward getting burnout because you want to do so much. Often, doing that much work is not healthy, and you can reach your limit pretty quickly—this results in burnout (HelpGuide, 2018).

How to Deal With Burnout and Emotional Fatigue

Often, it is hard to stop burnout in its tracks because you barely notice it happening to you until it's too late. Whenever you're feeling burnout, do not try to power through it and continue living the same lifestyle; you will only hurt yourself more both emotionally and physically. When you realize that you've reached your breaking point and you just can't take it anymore, you should stop whatever you're doing and think about how you can change your circumstances to prevent more damage from happening to you.

You need to learn how you can overcome burnout and do things again in a healthy way.

One of the best approaches to dealing with burnout is the 'Three R" approach. The three R's stand for recognize, reverse, and resilience.

You need to recognize the signs and symptoms of burnout. These signs are there to warn you to change your ways before you make things worse for yourself. Reverse the damage done by getting help and managing stress. The more support you have, the better you feel. Lastly, build your resilience. You need to make yourself more resilient to stress, and you can only do this by making sure you're healthy both physically and emotionally (HelpGuide, 2018).

You can also use the following tips to help you deal with burnout better.

Get Help and Support From Other People

When you reach the point of burnout, it could seem like your problems keep piling up, and you're getting crushed under their weight. You can't find a life preserver that can pull you out of the hole you seem to be falling in, and you can't even be bothered enough to care because you simply have no energy.

However, you're not as helpless as you think. You can control how stressed you feel in life. There are certain things you can do overall that can help you cope with the stress and allow you to put your life back on track. One of the greatest ways to do this is getting support from other people. Don't be afraid to reach out.

Human beings are not designed by nature to be solitary animals. We thrive off companionship and feel the best when we have a sense of community and a support system. Talking to somebody who is truly hearing out your problems is one of the quickest and best ways to alleviate stress and relax your nervous system. All this person has to do is listen; they don't have to give you a solution or try to fix your problem. Just find a good listener who will let you vent without any judgment. It will make you feel a lot better (HelpGuide, 2018).

You can do this by (HelpGuide, 2018):

- **Talking to Your Loved Ones:** These include your family, friends, or your significant other. You won't be imposing if you open up to them. These people will appreciate the fact that you trust them enough to share your problems with them. It will only make your bond stronger. Even if you don't want to discuss the negative feelings in your mind, just spending quality time with them can help you feel better.

- **Don't Cut Off Your Colleagues:** A lot of us have friendships at work that help us get through the day. Not having a friend at work can make the job seem even harder. Some of us have the mindset that we go to work not to make friends but that is wrong. A friend at work can help you decompress; they can act as a buffer between you and occupational burnout. Talk to your co-workers, grab lunch together, go out for coffee after work, or simply indulge in some water cooler gossip. It will make your job seem like a much happier and more fun place.

- **Delete Toxic People From Your Life:** People who are toxic never want what's best for you. They're always complaining and seeking some form of attention. You end up feeling drained after interacting with them. These people are always negative and can be serious downers. If you have no choice and you have to work with or be around toxic people, avoid spending any further time with them than you have to.

- **Find a Meaningful Activity or Support a Cause:** We all have certain causes that we feel passionately about. Maybe you want to help improve the plight of poor children, or you're passionate about rescuing animals. You can join a community of like-minded people and do something meaningful in your life. You can also become a part of a community that shares the same ideology you have. This could be religious, cultural, social, or just a support group. There are so many support groups present out there, both online and in person. You can join these communities to share your problems, get advice on how to handle stress, and make new friends in the process. These communities are usually welcoming and nonjudgmental so they can make you feel like you have a place in the world and give you a sense of purpose.

- **Make New Friends:** As we grow older, the prospect of making new friends becomes more challenging. We usually don't have the time or means to expand our social circle. However, times have now changed. You can make a lot of new, like-minded friends online. You can also befriend people by doing group activities. Take a yoga class or join a gym—talk to people there. Making new friends can bring a fresh perspective to your life, which could be a refreshing change for people experiencing burnout.

Change Your Approach Toward Work

Working the same tedious job for a long period can cause occupational burnout. Occupational burnout can happen due to a lot of reasons. You could be working somewhere where you don't feel appreciated or valued. It can also happen if you have a very fast-paced job where you're always rushing or if your job is very tedious and repetitive.

The easiest way to avoid occupational burnout is to quit the job that's giving you grief, and find something that you enjoy and are passionate about doing. However, switching jobs is not always a feasible option. We need to make money and pay the bills, and often, our dream job is not something offered to us just because we want it. Still, it's not impossible and can be done. Even if you can't switch jobs, there are still things you can do to avoid getting occupational burnout. These include (HelpGuide, 2018):

- **Trying to Find Meaning and Value In Your Job:** All jobs have a purpose, otherwise, it wouldn't be a job. Even if your job seems the most pointless, boring, and monotonous, try to figure out how your job contributes to the world and how it helps other people. For instance, do you provide a service to other people that they need or enjoy? Do you sell a product that helps make people's lives easier? Try to focus on the parts of your job that you like. It can be something as basic as having lunch with your favorite co-worker. Change your perspective; look at your job from a different perspective so that you can get back your control and your sense of purpose.

- **Live a Balanced Life:** Try to create a balance in your life. If there is one part of your life that you're unhappy with, you should look at the other parts of your life which make you happy. Do you have meaningful relationships? They can help offset a lack of meaning in your work life and vice versa. Try to appreciate the good things in your life.

- **Talk to People at Work:** Making friends at work is a good way to prevent occupational workout. Having someone to talk to who is going through the same experiences as you can really help a challenging workplace seem more tolerable. You should talk to your colleagues and get to know their hobbies and interests. You might find a new friendship that you really enjoy. It will help you from feeling overwhelmed by work and give you an outlet to decompress.

- **Go On Vacation:** If you feel exhaustion and fatigue creeping up on you, it's time to take a break. Even if you can't go internationally or to another city, just take a break in your city. Go to the beach, an amusement park, or go watch a movie. Use your sick days; ask for time off. Do whatever you need to do to get some space and break away from the situation. Utilize your time off to rejuvenate yourself and gain your energy back.

Reassess Your Priorities

If your life has reached the point of burnout, it's your body's way of telling you that there is something in your life that just isn't working out for you. Take a good hard look at your life. Are you working on achieving your hopes and dreams or have you let that get away from you? Are you ignoring something important to you? Think about what makes you happy and let yourself rest and heal.

You can do this by (HelpGuide, 2018):

- **Establishing Boundaries for Yourself:** Not having boundaries can spread you thin. You need to learn how to stand up for yourself. There's nothing wrong with being assertive and establishing boundaries. A lot of people feel guilty saying no, but you shouldn't. Remember that when you say no to things you don't want to do, you're allowing yourself to say yes to things you do want to do.

- **Disconnect:** These days, we're constantly connected which can cause sensory overload. We're taking in so many opinions and content that we don't even realize what's going on in our minds. All of this can eventually end up exhausting you. You should set a time in the day where you completely disconnect from all technology. Switch off your phone, turn off the laptop, and sign out of social media. A good idea to do this is to disconnect an hour before you go to bed. This way, you can get a good night's sleep without getting disrupted by notifications.

- **Have a Creative Outlet:** When you have a creative outlet, it can help take a lot of stress off your shoulders. If you don't already have a creative outlet, take up something that appeals to you. Do you enjoy working with your hands? Take something apart and put it together again. Do an arts and crafts project or write a story. Maybe learn how to play a musical instrument. Select something that seems fun and doesn't seem like work.

- **Schedule Relaxation Time:** Set aside some time in the day where you just relax. Have a hot cup of tea or a refreshing drink and just chill out. Maybe lie down and watch some TV. Maybe try some deep breathing techniques or meditate. You shouldn't do anything else during that hour but relax. The whole point of this is to get your body into a state of relaxation. Chilling out like this triggers your body's relaxation response so it can help you offset the stress response.

- **Don't Skip Sleep:** Make sure you get a full night's sleep. Not sleeping can amp up feelings of stress and can mess with your mind by making you think irrationally. This can help you combat feelings of stress.

Be Active and Exercise

When you're experiencing burnout, getting any form of exercise can seem like a Herculean task. Since you're so low energy, you don't feel like getting up from your bed much less work out.

However, exercise is one of the best ways to combat stress and burnout. You can always get off your bed and work out a little; just break out of the monotony, and get out of your head. This could help improve your mood a lot.

Set exercise goals for yourself. Try to get at least 30 minutes of exercise every day. You don't have to work out for 30 minutes altogether. You can do short exercises for 10 minutes throughout the day. Exercises don't mean you have to pick up weights or do push-ups or crunches. You could just take a walk, a swim, or stretch. Just walking for 10 minutes can improve your mood for a couple of hours.

One of the most effective ways to boost your mood is by doing rhythmic exercise. Rhythmic exercises require you to move both your arms and legs. These include swimming, running, dancing, walking, and martial arts. By doing this type of exercise, you get a serious energy boost, and this can help make you feel more focused. Most importantly, it helps relax you completely in both your mind and your body.

During exercise, you can shift your focus from your negative thoughts to the sensations your body is experiencing as it moves. This helps you bust stress and helps prevent and combat burnout (HelpGuide, 2018).

These tips help you deal with burnout. Let's now discuss ways that you can help combat stress.

Chapter 6:

How to Stop Stress In Its Tracks

We all get stressed in life. Chronic stress can be seriously debilitating. However, that does not mean you should consider being stressed as an acceptable state of mind. You can't help getting stressed. Your body's stress response kicks in after being exposed to stressors. However, you can influence how long your body remains stressed.

You can take steps to stop stress in its tracks and prevent it from consuming you.

Here are 10 things you can do to stop stress in its tracks.

The 10 Things to Stop Stress In Its Tracks

#1: Don't Let Your Mind Wander

Have you ever heard the expression that you're "thinking yourself dizzy?" Well, you can think of yourself as more stressful as well. We all face numerous stressors in our day-to-day routines. It's normal to ponder over these stressful factors in our lives and wonder how we can change things and improve upon them. However, some of us tend to get a bit obsessive and constantly keep our minds on these stressors. This is not healthy; it is extremely negative. This type of myopic, obsessive thinking can make your stress more intense because you're constantly playing these stressful thoughts in your mind like a movie. Don't!

When we get stuck in this vicious thought cycle, we tend to focus more on the things that went wrong rather than try to find a solution.

The good thing is that you can break this bad habit. Whenever you feel like you're obsessing over something negative, make a conscious effort to shift your thoughts to something less unpleasant. Distract yourself. Read a book, turn on the TV, or call a friend and change the topic. Sometimes, even changing your environment slightly can help break the pattern. If you're lying on your bed obsessing over all the stressors in your life, get up and walk around the house. Doing these conscious things to break the obsessive thought pattern will help you deal with stress much better. (Scott, 2019)

#2: *Avoid Self-Sabotage*

We all have an inner saboteur that tells us we're not good enough and sets us up to fail. You need to learn how to tell that saboteur to shut up and have a good enough sense of self-worth to know that you are good enough; while it's perfectly natural to feel nervous or second guess yourself from time to time, you should never buy what your inner saboteur is trying to sell you because that is the worst part of yourself (Scott, 2019).

#3: *Stop Cognitive Distortions*

Cognitive distortions mean a messed up or distorted way of thinking. We can become so used to thinking a certain way that it becomes difficult to imagine there ever could be an alternate way of thinking. Our thoughts shape how we see the world around us, and obviously, this has a great impact on our stress level. This can be a good thing if you're a naturally positive person, but if you're negatively inclined, you could invite stress into your life. This happens because the stress response in our body only activates when we perceive a threat—perception being the key word. When we feel threatened, our bodies believe we are being threatened and activate stress mode, so you need to change the way you think and stop inviting stress into your life (Scott, 2019).

#4: *Change Your Environment*

When we feel stressed, we can feel trapped and claustrophobic. Whenever we feel overwhelmed and under a lot of pressure, we can feel suffocated by our surroundings. If you feel like you're starting to get stressed, you can stop stress in its tracks by removing yourself from your surroundings. Just get up and go somewhere else. Maybe take a walk outside or go to the park. Go to the beach if you have access to one. If you're not a very outdoorsy person, go to the mall or get some ice cream. Even going from one room to the next can help. If you have a garden or a terrace, step out and spend some time there. Studies have shown that being outdoors in nature can help reduce cortisol levels in your body. Remember the saying; "fresh air will do you good?" It's true! Getting fresh air and changing your scenery helps calm you down because it alleviates the stress hormones in your body. Go figure (Hogan,

2017)!

#5: Don't Ponder Over the Past or the Future

Generally, when we are stressed or experiencing anxiety, we are worried about what could happen to us or fixated about controlling the future. Worrying doesn't solve anything, and it's not a pleasant state of mind to be in. Dr. Tamar Chansky, author of the book *Freeing Yourself from Anxiety* and also a PhD and psychologist, says that there is absolutely no point worrying about what could happen; especially because we have no control over the future, and neither are we clairvoyant. Instead, she suggests that we should pull ourselves back to the present and focus on what is happening now rather than worry about what could happen to us later (Hughes, 2017).

Fretting over the past is useless as well. You can't go back and change what happened; the best you can do is learn from it and move on. (Hughes, 2017)

#6: Change the Narrative

Oftentimes, how we perceive a situation determines how badly or positively it affects us. For example, if you've just won a prize, you could think how excited you are and narrate what happened in your mind as positive. However, you could also think that when you just won a prize, you question whether it's real or a scam. You could also doubt the reason why you won. That is creating a negative narrative about what is happening. You get to decide the narrative. Why would you choose to go negative? You have the power. Relabel what is happening around you to help cope with the situation better. For example, when a person is having a panic attack, they can feel like they are dying. If you think you're going to die, you're going to end up exacerbating the panic attack even more. If you tell yourself, "I know I'm having a panic attack. It will soon pass; it can't harm me," you can calm down much sooner. Besides, a panic attack indicates the exact opposite of death. Your body is kicking into the fight-or-flight response because it wants to survive and stay alive (Hughes, 2017)!

#7: *Verify Your Thoughts*

In the age of fake news, verification is pretty important. Did you know this concept applies to your thoughts, too? If you're suffering from anxiety or under immense stress, you might have a habit of fixating on the worst possible outcome of any situation. This kind of nihilistic thinking only contributes to your stress. To alleviate the stress from this situation, you need to consider how realistic your fears are. If you're convinced you're going to mess up a major work assignment and tell yourself, "I'm going to mess up," verify the truth of that statement. Check your thoughts and then come back with the real statement which can be something like, "I've worked hard on this assignment. I might mess up, but I'll likely do okay."

Once you develop a habit of thinking this way, you can train your brain to deal with your stressful and anxious thoughts logically and rationally (Hughes, 2017).

#8: Practice Deep Breathing

Deep breathing is a tried-and-true method of stopping stress in its tracks. Some therapists might recommend specific breathing exercises, but that's not important. You just breathe deeply, in and out, in whichever way that feels comfortable to you. Whenever you feel your body tensing up and getting stressed, or whenever you feel like you're starting to get overwhelmed, just take a second and breathe. Breathe deeply, in through your nose, hold it for a couple of seconds, and then out through your mouth. Don't think about anything else during this time: Just concentrate on breathing in and out. Inhale and then slowly exhale. Some people like to count to 10, but again, that's not important. You should breathe deeply for however long it takes you to settle down. Deep breathing is so effective because it helps calm your mind so you can focus again on the task at hand (Hughes, 2017).

#9: Do the 3-3-3

What is the 3-3-3? The 3-3-3 rule is a method you can employ that helps stop stress in its tracks. It's not very complicated either. All you have to do is look around the room and name any three things you see. For example, you take a look around your bedroom and see your bed, a chair, and your desk, so you say, "bed, chair, desk" out loud. Then, you should name any three sounds you hear. For example, in your room you could hear the TV, the wind, and the cat meowing, so you say, "TV, wind, cat." Lastly, you should move any three parts of your body, such as your wrist, your leg, or your fingers.

It might seem lame, but it's very effective at calming down racing thoughts. Whenever you feel restless, anxious, and on edge, this technique can help center you and help you relax (Hughes, 2017).

#10: Just Do Something . . . ANYTHING

When we feel stressed or anxious, the best thing we can do at that time is to break that stressful chain of thoughts coiling around our brain and squeezing it tight. All you have to do is . . . well, anything.

You could stand up if you're sitting, or sit down if you're standing. You could arrange your desk, clean up your space, or simply go wash your face. When you take conscious action to disrupt stressful thoughts, you take back your power and regain control (Hughes, 2017).

These strategies can help you stop stress in its tracks. You must have heard the saying that "Prevention is better than cure." These tips will help you avoid getting stressed out in the first place. Stress only gets deadly when it keeps building up and you have no outlet for release. The best thing you can do is to identify your stress triggers, recognize that you're getting stressed, and stop it from building up; the techniques mentioned in this chapter will help with that.

We now know that stress is a physiological, emotional, and mental response, but did you know that what you eat can impact your stress levels in a major way?

In the next chapter, we will discuss the impact nutrition has on our stress levels.

Chapter 7:

Cook Up a Stress-Free Life

We've all heard the saying, "You are what you eat." This statement is so true—in more ways than one. What we eat plays such a huge role in determining not only our physical health but our mental health as well. Scientists are discovering deeper connections between nutrition and mental health every single day, and the level of impact nutrition has on our stress levels can surprise you.

Let's first address the question of whether food has an impact on our mental health or not.

Does Food Affect Our Mental Health?

Scientists don't always agree on everything, but almost every credible scientist and health researcher agrees that what we eat is very important for our physical and mental health. Over the years, there has been so much debate over what is considered to be a healthy diet. For example, in the 80s, being fat-free was all the rage. Now, we have discovered that fat is good for us, and it is sugar that is bad for us. Food science and nutritional science are always evolving, but what is established is that what we eat has a big impact on our health.

We always knew that what we ate determines how physically healthy we are. You cannot have a diet that comprises fast food and soda and expect to be healthy. However, we have just started to collect evidence that a bad diet can be bad for our mental health as well. The journal, *European Neuropsychopharmacology*, recently published an article that explains the connection between nutrition and our mental well-being and mood extensively.

What the article said makes a lot of sense. It explains that our brain is an organ like our heart and our liver. Our organs rely on proper nutrition for their smooth functioning and so does the brain. The brain's structure, composition, and function are utterly reliant on nutrients to work properly. What we eat has an impact on our mind, our mental health, and our mood. It suggests that people who suffer from mental health issues like anxiety, depression, and even epilepsy could see an improvement in their conditions if they change their diets (Frye, 2020).

A lot of credible scientific reviews found that people who eat a diet full of lean proteins, whole grains, and a lot of fruits and vegetables tend to have better control over their mood. They generally report feeling happier and are usually in a good mood. It has been theorized that such a diet can even help alleviate the severity of depression symptoms (Frye, 2020).

They also believe that special diet plans can help improve the symptoms of certain mental health disorders. Many credible pieces of research show that children who suffer from epilepsy can benefit from being on the ketogenic diet, which eliminates carbohydrates and only allows gaining calories from protein and fat (Frye, 2020).

Poor nutrition can even cause poor mental health. Medical professionals have known about how a vitamin B12 deficiency can cause poor memory, lethargy, fatigue, depression, and can also cause the one suffering from it to develop mania and psychosis (Frye, 2020).

The importance of prenatal vitamins and supplements is known to every medical professional. Pregnant women need an abundance of vitamins and minerals to ensure the proper development of their babies. Folic acid is essential for a pregnant woman. If a pregnant woman has a folic acid deficiency, her baby can get depression as an adult! Imagine, something that your mother didn't have when she was pregnant can adversely affect you in your adult life! If we don't get enough niacin, we are more prone to getting dementia.

The connection between nutrition and cognitive function is obvious. Researchers have found clear evidence that what we eat now can impact our mental health later on in life. We still are not clear about how exactly this happens, but it does happen. Scientists have found that people who adhere to the Mediterranean diet have improved brain function later in life. This is because this diet is rich in whole foods and lean proteins, and it eliminates all processed foods and sugars. They have also discovered that individuals who eat a diet that is full of sugar and trans fat have impaired cognitive function (Frye, 2020).

The link between nutrition and mental health is evident. But how does our diet correlate to stress?

How a Bad Diet Can Cause Stress

A lot of us turn to food for comfort. There are certain types of foods that are considered "comfort food" because we reach for those things when we feel stressed. However, certain foods end up causing us to become more stressed because they add to the strain our body is feeling instead of alleviating it.

Some types of food add to our stress and anxiety because they do not provide our body with all the necessary nutrients that we need. They can end up causing inflammation and putting more strain on our body's natural physiological systems and can elevate the levels of stress hormones in our body.

Here is a list of foods that can cause you to become more stressed:

White Flour

White flour is processed. Processed food is not always bad, but in this case, the processing strips most of the nutrients from the flour. Flour naturally is rich in fiber and has a lot of germ and bran, but these nutrients end up getting lost in the process.

White flour is refined, which means it's missing its outer layer. This outer layer is the most fibrous and nutritious. Refined flour gets digested very quickly and then rapidly absorbed by the bloodstream. This can cause our blood sugar levels to spike up, triggering the release of cortisol into our bodies, which causes stress.

The bad news is products made from white flour are delicious, so it's very easy to eat a lot of it. We love eating white bread, white rice, and a whole range of other delicious baked goods. If you don't want to eat a lot of white flour, you might want to start reading nutrition labels. Choose products that are made from unrefined flour instead. This is because unrefined carbs don't cause drastic changes in your blood sugar. Unrefined carbohydrates include brown rice, bran, and quinoa.

If you love white flour, you can have it in moderation. Consider it a treat rather than a meal. If you must have white flour, it's a good idea to have it with goods that are rich in fiber such as vegetables. This would help reduce the rate of absorption in your bloodstream (Kramer, 2019).

Salt

Wait a minute . . . salt? We can't be expected to eat bland food! Well, you're not. A small amount of salt is fine, but if you're used to adding a lot of salt to flavor your meals, you can cause an excess of sodium to build up in your body. Having a lot of sodium in your body can make you bloated and cause fluid retention, which in turn can cause your blood pressure to shoot up and cause hypertension. These symptoms can put a lot of strain on your heart.

High blood pressure, hypertension, and rapid heartbeat are all symptoms of stress. Sodium contributes to these symptoms. You must keep your sodium levels low if you want to keep your stress levels down. The ideal amount of salt you should consume every day is less than 2,300 mg (Kramer, 2019).

To make sure you stay within the limit, you'll have to add less salt to the food you cook at home, and when you're buying groceries, try to choose the low-sodium options for packaged foods. You can also try to make your snacks at home to avoid buying processed items with a lot of sodium (Kramer, 2019).

Processed Meats

Meat in itself is not bad for you—it's meat that goes through processing that is harmful. A lot of people joke about hot dogs and nuggets being mystery meat, and actually, they are not wrong. Processed meats like sausages, deli meats, and beef jerky contain a lot of additives that might not be the healthiest and can be the cause of stress.

Manufacturers add a lot of preservatives to these processed meats which make them taste better and last longer on supermarket shelves. These include a lot of sodium and other additives that can cause remarkable drops in your energy level and can make you more stressed.

It's really hard to remove processed meats from our diet

because they are so deeply integrated into our lives. We eat hot dogs at games and barbecues, we add deli meat to our sandwiches, and a lot of us eat bacon for breakfast. However, that's just setting us up for more stress. Instead of eating processed meat, we should choose whole-food sources of animal products. Opt for slices of fresh meat, choose leaner cuts of white meat such as turkey and chicken, and incorporate fish into your diet (Kramer, 2019).

Sugar

Sugar is the biggest dietary culprit, responsible for causing obesity, diabetes, and yes, even stress. We never even think about the fact that as we enjoy a cool soda or have a piece of cake that the sugar in these foods is causing the cortisol levels in our body to skyrocket! Sugar increases the level of cortisol in our bodies, causing us to become more stressed.

If we have a diet that is high in sugary foods, our body's blood sugar levels will always be unstable. Unstable sugar levels put a lot of stress on the body, which means that there will be a lot of cortisol present in our system to deal with this mess. When we have unstable blood sugar and a lot of cortisol in the body, it's a recipe for feeling stressed out and anxious.

The recommended level of sugar intake varies in women and men. Men should not have more than nine teaspoons of sugar a day, while women should have a maximum of six teaspoons of sugar every day (Kramer, 2019).

If you want to stop eating a lot of sugar, the first thing you need to do is figure out which of our foods contain sugar. So many of our foods contain hidden sugars. You need to find where sugar lurks in these foods and get rid of them from your diet. You'd be surprised to learn that even foods that don't taste sweet have sugar. Even fruits and vegetables have sugar. If there's sugar in everything, how do we escape it?

Read the label on packaged products, and search online for which foods have sugar in them. Fruits and vegetables contain natural sugars which are not as bad for you as white sugar. However, sodas, coffee drinks, condiments, salad dressings, cereals, and prepackaged yogurts all have a lot of sugar. Read the labels and choose foods that don't have a high percentage of sugar, and if you do eat very sugary food, try not to consume any more sugar for the rest of the day (Kramer, 2019).

Caffeine

A lot of us believe that we need caffeine to get through the day. There are so many of us that can't function until we get that morning cup of coffee. Sure, caffeine makes you feel energized. How? It increases levels of cortisol in your body. The energy you feel is produced because when you're stressed, your energy levels spike up.

Caffeine can also cause your blood pressure to rise and your heartbeat to quicken. What do these symptoms remind you of? Maybe the symptoms of the fight-or-flight response we discussed in a previous chapter? As caffeine causes your cortisol levels to rise, you can end up feeling more stressed and anxious after consuming it. Caffeine also limits the rate of absorption of nutrients that can help improve your moods such as vitamin D and B. Not only is it causing stress but it is taking away nutrients that help alleviate stress.

Caffeine can also cause insomnia which leads to more stress. A good night's sleep is essential otherwise you can experience burnout and or fatigue-related stress.

You don't need to cut coffee and other sources of caffeine entirely from your diet. How would we get through the day otherwise, right? You just have to limit how much caffeine you consume. You can't have more than two cups of coffee a day, and try to avoid drinking more than one caffeinated beverage in a day such as a flavored latte, any energy drink, or another caffeinated beverage.

If you're feeling ambitious or have caffeine sensitivity, you can also try to cut caffeine entirely from your diet. You can swap the coffee for green tea, juice, or any other healthy, decaffeinated drink (Kramer, 2019).

Fried Foods

Yes, French fries taste divine. Unfortunately, fries and other fried foods can cause you to become more stressed out. Sounds unfair, but it's true.

If you eat a lot of fried food, it can cause a serious drop in your energy levels. Many people who have a diet rich in fast food end up leading pretty sedentary lifestyles, which is extremely unhealthy. You feel uncomfortable, sluggish, and slow most of the time, and it takes away your motivation to be active. This causes more stress and mimics the symptoms of burnout.

If you've ever noticed, people who eat a lot of fast food tend to be morbidly obese and lead pretty sedentary lifestyles. They don't like moving around a lot, and their bodies slowly become a cage for them. This type of lifestyle can be pretty stressful.

Instead of having a lot of fried foods, explore other types of food and alternative cooking methods. Grilled, steamed, baked, sautéed, and roasted foods can taste just as good. If you simply love fried food and crave it, try finding a healthier option like getting an air fryer. That way, you can enjoy the same food with less oil and grease, which means you'd be less likely to get stressed (Kramer, 2019)!

Alcohol

Most of us drink alcohol to unwind. We come home from a fairly long day at work and grab a beer. We drink to de-stress because alcohol is a mild sedative. This means that it can make us calm for a short time. However, if we drink too much, we can end up making our stress and anxiety much worse, especially if we're already prone to experiencing it.

This is because alcohol reduces the level of serotonin in the body. Serotonin is the hormone that makes us happy and puts us in a good mood. When alcohol reduces the serotonin in our body, we can end up feeling stressed and sad.

So how much is too much drinking? According to the Centers for Disease Control and Prevention, anything more than two drinks a day for men and one drink a day for women is too much (Kramer, 2019). If you drink more than this amount, you're putting pressure on your liver to metabolize more alcohol than it can handle at once. This means that the extra alcohol will be circulating in your bloodstream until your liver has room for it.

If you feel you drink too much, you can cut back by avoiding places and people that trigger your drinking. Spend your time doing other things you enjoy instead of drinking. There are plenty of things you can do without involving alcohol. Go to the mall, hang out with a friend, or go to the gym.

It does feel good to come home after a long day of work and sip something. It doesn't have to be booze. Instead of grabbing that beer, grab a smoothie or some tea with honey and lemon to sip on. Herbal teas like chamomile and lavender have marvelous calming effects. Opt for these, and they will help you de-stress instead of alcohol, which just gives you the illusion of de-stressing (Kramer, 2019).

The fact is that a lot of the foods mentioned here taste good and feel good, so, understandably, you wouldn't want to quit them. You don't have to. These foods are only bad for you and can cause you to stress if you consume them regularly. Consuming these foods in moderation and every once in a while is fine—it's having them excessively that can become problematic.

Avoiding foods that cause stress is one way to keep stress and anxiety at bay. There are many other simple techniques that you can incorporate in your life which will prevent you from feeling stressed out.

We will discuss those in the next chapter.

Chapter 8:

Simple Ways to Relieve Anxiety and Stress

Sometimes, the stress in our lives can seem very overpowering, and we feel helpless when confronted with it. However, it is very important to remember that while you might be feeling anxious, tired, frustrated, or sad, the one thing that you are NOT is helpless.

You always have the power to change your current mental state no matter how stressful it is. The stressors that we have to deal with in our day-to-day life can take a toll on us, but it is up to us whether we let them defeat us or not.

Being stressed is a part of life. Everybody feels stressed; life wouldn't be life as we know it if we didn't. However, it is how we cope with this stress that determines how successful we are at managing our lives. A little bit of stress can help us. It can motivate us, energize us, and give us that little extra push we need to accomplish our goals.

However, excessive and chronic stress is debilitating and can seriously affect our quality of life. It can even end up being lethal.

We learned in a previous chapter how to stop stress in its tracks. In this chapter, we will learn 20 simple techniques that we can use to alleviate stress. If you incorporate these techniques into your daily life, you'd be able to cope with stressful situations much easier and hopefully lead a more carefree life.

The 20 Simple Ways You Can Reduce Stress

#1: Be More Active

We have talked about the importance of exercise extensively in this book, but it bears repeating because it is just that impactful when it comes to alleviating stress.

People often get confused because they say, "How is putting more stress on my body going to help me reduce stress?" Physical stress can help alleviate mental stress pretty quickly. You can see the benefits when you keep exercising. Those of us who work out more frequently tend to be less anxious than people who don't.

The main reason behind this is because exercise reduces the overall level of cortisol in your body and produces endorphins that make you happy. Regularly exercising can help you get better sleep. When you work out, you look good, so you feel more confident which improves your mental health! It's a win-win scenario.

#2: Get Supplements

Supplements are quite beneficial for alleviating stress. Here is a list of common supplements that you might want to try to reduce stress (Krans, 2018):

- **Lemon balm** has proven anti-anxiety effects.

- **Omega-3 fatty acids** reduce stress levels and anxiety symptoms.

- **Ashwagandha** is an ancient herb used to treat anxiety and stress.

- **Green tea** increases serotonin and contains antioxidants.

- **Valerian** helps you sleep and makes you calm.

- **Kava kava** is a sedative used to treat mild stress and anxiety.

#3: Get Scented Candles

Scented candles work wonders for your mood and help reduce stress. You can get scented candles infused with essential oils that help soothe stress. Some of the most effective scents include rose, lavender, sandalwood, orange blossom, chamomile, bergamot, geranium, frankincense, and coconut.

#4: Write Your Feelings Down

Keeping a journal can help you vent out feelings of stress and frustration and can also help you gain perspective into why you were feeling that way. It can help you focus on what is positive in your life.

#5: Chew Gum

Researchers have found that people who habitually chew gum have lower stress levels and generally feel good, and they have a better sense of well-being than most (Krans, 2018). This could be because the act of chewing gum produces brain waves that mimic feelings of relaxation and because chewing gum increases blood flow to the brain.

#6: Socialize

When we spend time with people we like, our bodies release oxytocin—the love hormone. It naturally relieves stress and causes the "tend-and-befriend" response, which is the direct opposite of the fight-or-flight response (Krans, 2018).

#7: Laugh

Laughter is the best medicine for a reason. Laughing relaxes your muscles, which relieves the strain from your muscles. It also settles the stress response, making you calmer.

#8: Say "No"

You need to learn how and when to say "no" more often. When you say no, you're taking control of your stressors by refusing to take on more responsibility than you can handle.

#9: Don't Procrastinate

When you procrastinate, you end up reacting to an urgent situation by rushing to complete something that could have calmly been done if it was on time. This causes stress. Avoid stress by completing your work on time.

#10: Do Yoga

Yoga is one of the best ways to relieve stress. Yoga is a combination of deep breathing, stretching, mindfulness, and deliberate body movements. It de-stresses every part of your body, lowers cortisol levels, blood pressure, and heart rate. It also produces GABA neurotransmitters that stabilize your mood (Krans, 2018).

#11: Be Mindful

Learn some mindfulness exercises and practice them. Mindfulness makes you aware of the present and helps center you when you feel lost. It helps you deal with negative thoughts that can cause anxiety.

#12: Cuddle and Kiss

Positive physical touch, like cuddling, kissing, and even sex can help reduce stress drastically. This is because these actions reduce cortisol levels and increase the production of oxytocin, which makes you happy and calm.

#13: Listen to Calming Music

Soothing music (anything slow and calming) induces your body's relaxation response which combats the stress response in your body.

#14: Practice Deep Breathing

This is a tried and tested way of reducing stress which can be done anywhere at any time.

#15: Take a Bath

A warm bath can really help soothe frazzled nerves. You can consider this as your "me time." Go all out; light a scented candle, use a nice bath bomb, put in some bubble bath, and go in with your favorite book, calming music, or a podcast. When you relax, your brain signals the rest of your body to calm down as well. Take out an hour or 45 minutes and just relax among the soap suds.

#16: Go Out in the Sun

Sunlight is a very good way to alleviate symptoms of depression. It literally helps "chase the blues away." It helps because bright light has been connected to improving a bad mood. Plus, you get a good dose of vitamin D, too. Just don't stay out too long, and make sure you take the SPF with you!

#17: Rub Your Feet Over a Golf Ball

This might seem weird but it's actually quite effective. All you have to do is sit on a comfortable chair or sofa and put a golf ball under your bare feet. Then you roll the ball with your feet. This acts like a makeshift foot massage and it provides a calming effect. It's also great for aching feet!

#18: Squeeze a Stress Ball

Sometimes, when you feel the rage and frustration building up inside you and you want to slap somebody silly, just take a stress ball and squeeze it hard. It's a quick, legal, and violent way to get out those angry feelings. Plus, it really works!

#19: Give Progressive Relaxation a Shot

Progressive relaxation means making the muscles tense in your body one part at a time. Just squeeze and release. Start with your fingers, then work your way down your feet and legs. This allows you to concentrate on the movements and diverts your mind from the stress. You are consciously unclenching the tensed muscles in your body. This is signaling your brain to let go of the stress, quite literally, so you feel much calmer and relaxed.

#20: Hang Out With Your Pet

Hanging out with your pet, cuddling them, and playing with them is a great way to release stress. Spending time with your pet also releases oxytocin, which makes you happy and calm (Krans, 2018).

You can use these simple techniques whenever you're feeling stressed out, and they will make you calm and relaxed. They are very easy to do, and you can pretty much do them whenever you feel the need to. None of these methods are difficult to obtain and can help you out when you're feeling stressed.

Even though the methods mentioned above are effective and are medically endorsed, they are not exactly medically designed techniques for stress relief. We will discuss those techniques in the next chapter.

Chapter 9:

Scientifically Proven Stress-Relief Techniques

We have established by now that there are many reasons why people get stressed and why their symptoms progressively get worse. Medical professionals have worked extensively to discover stress-management techniques that can help people who are suffering from chronic stress and stress-related disorders to get some relief and be able to cope with the stresses in their lives in a much healthier way.

We will discuss some of the most effective, scientifically endorsed stress-management techniques in this chapter.

Medically Endorsed Stress-Management Techniques

The 4 A's

The 4 A's are a part of a stress management strategy designed to guide us when we're experiencing a stressful situation.

This is what the 4 A's stand for:

Avoid

Did you know you can simply avoid getting stressed? It's not as easy as it might sound but it can be done. All you have to do is identify where your stress is coming from. Then do the following:

- Take control of your surroundings.

- Don't meet people who stress you out.

- Don't be afraid to say "no."

- Shuffle your list of things to do.

These steps will help you avoid taking on stress to begin with. However, if that's not an option, then you can move on to the next A. (Clinics, 2020)

Alter

If you are not able to avoid the situation, then do your best to alter or change it. Take a good look at the situation that's stressing you out and then try to change it to work better for you. How?

- Ask the person stressing you out to change their behavior
- Don't be afraid to share your feelings
- Manage time more efficiently
- Make your boundaries and limitations clear

Most of the time, you'd be able to alter the situation to help you reduce stress. However, if you can't, move on to the next step (Horizon Clinics, 2020).

Accept

When you have no power over a situation; you can't avoid it or change it, you simply have to accept it. Accepting that you can't do anything about a certain situation can make you realize that stressing about it is just not worth it.

The following steps can help you accept things more easily:

- Share your feelings.
- Forgive others.
- Build yourself up with positive self-talk.
- Learn from your mistakes.

Sometimes, acceptance alone doesn't cut it. You have to figure out how to make the situation work for you, and this means you adapt to it, which is our final A (Horizon Clinics, 2020).

Adapt

When you try to adapt to a difficult situation, you can help turn the situation in your favor. You can always change your expectations, even if you can't change anything else. Here are steps you can take that will help you adapt more easily:

- Have flexible standards and expectations.
- Practice thought reversal.
- Relabel your issue.
- Have an affirmation and follow it.
- Look at the big picture.

There you have it. The 4 A's can help you defuse stressful situations and help you adapt even when things seem difficult

(Horizon Clinics, 2020). There are other medically endorsed stress-management techniques you can use as well.

Short-Term Stress-Management Techniques

Short-term stress-management techniques help you deal with acute stress. You could be feeling particularly stressed out at a certain point during your day and using these techniques can help alleviate that stress. These include (Horizon Clinics, 2020):

- **Meditation:** Meditation helps you center your thoughts and calm yourself. It gives you a better sense of purpose and makes you feel more connected to yourself. It is great for alleviating stress. If you don't know how to meditate on your own, you can go to YouTube and pull up guided meditation videos which will help you get started.

- **Walking:** Any exercise is good for stress relief, but walking is easy and simple and can be done at any time by anyone.

- **Deep Breathing:** As mentioned before, deep breathing alleviates stress by reducing levels of cortisol in your body. You take in more oxygen which relaxes rapid heartbeat during stressful times.

- **Guided Imagery:** Guided imagery uses positive and calming pictures with music to create pleasant imaginary scenarios in your mind. This is a great way to relieve stress. You can find guided imagery exercises on YouTube, as well (Scholle, 2015).

- **Practice Progressive Muscle Relaxation:** This means doing things that help release muscular tension. This could include getting a massage, stretching, using a hot or cold compress, or simply getting proper hydration.

Fast-Acting Stress-Management Techniques

Sometimes when we're feeling very stressed out and on the verge of having a panic attack, we need to practice some fast-acting stress-management techniques that help calm us down at that very moment. These include (Horizon Clinics, 2020):

- **Aromatherapy:** Breathing in pleasant smells from essential oils can be very calming and soothing. Chamomile, lavender, and sandalwood are just some essential oil scents that are known for their soothing, anti-anxiety properties.

- **Create Art:** People who are stressed can always turn to artwork to help alleviate that stress. Coloring, painting, and even working with dyes can help alleviate stress. You can do needlework embroidery, quilting, or give diamond painting a try.

- **A Hug:** Sometimes when we're stressed and frazzled, simply getting a hug from a loved one can help calm us down. Hugs release oxytocin into our bodies, making us happy and reducing stress.

Long-Term Stress-Management Techniques

These are techniques that you should make a part of your everyday life if you want to live a more carefree lifestyle. If you make a habit out of practicing these techniques, you're likely to be a much happier, more relaxed, and stress-free person. These techniques include (Horizon Clinics, 2020):

- **Yoga:** The stress-relieving properties of Yoga have been discussed extensively in previous chapters.

- **Exercise Daily:** As we know, exercise releases endorphins. The more endorphins we produce, the less stress we take on in our lives.

- **Show Gratitude:** Be thankful for the things you have instead of focusing on the things you don't. Be appreciative of what you have in life. This will make you more aware of all the good things in your life, rather than having to focus on the bad.

- **Eat a Balanced Diet:** The importance of good nutrition has been discussed extensively in "Chapter 7: Cook Up a Stress-Free Life."

- **Take Time Out for Fun:** You need to set some time apart every day for leisure activities. "Me time" helps you feel happier, calmer, and more relaxed, which is a guaranteed stress buster.

- **Get Cognitive Behavioral Therapy:** You will work with a therapist who will help you identify negative and unhealthy thoughts and help you replace them with positive ones (Harvard Health Publishing, 2015).

- **Use Positive Affirmations:** Look in the mirror every morning and tell yourself three things that you love and appreciate about yourself and your life. Say things like, "'I'm beautiful," "I love myself," and "I am happy." These will make you feel more confident and build up your self-esteem, making you a much happier and much less stressed out person!

You can choose to either follow all of these techniques or choose the technique which is right for you. If you are still not able to find relief from stress, it might be a good idea to go seek help from a professional therapist or a counselor.

Conclusion

A lot of people feel like being stressed is a normal part of life, so they resign themselves to their fate and just accept that they will have to go through life feeling stressed out and anxious. Nothing can be further from the truth!

Yes, being stressed is a normal part of life. Stress is an essential physiological response that can save your life. It is because of stress that you have the drive to get your work done, that you want to perform better, or that you compete and want to win.

However, excessive stress can be seriously debilitating, and the hope is that this book has taught you not to take chronic stress lightly. Excessive stress can be and has proven to be fatal, unfortunately, with many people dying either due to stress-related physical complications or by committing suicide.

Being stress-free is not an unattainable dream. It is a goal that you should aspire to achieve. Who doesn't want to live a carefree life?

It is at your disposal: You just need to put in a little work and effort.

It's all about shifting your mindset and accepting that you will not let yourself be a victim of your stress. You control the narrative of your life. You decide how you perceive stressful situations; you can let them defeat you, or you can conquer them and emerge victorious and stronger than ever.

All the stress management techniques mentioned in this book are very simple. You can easily incorporate them into your life. It is more about training your mind than training your body. These techniques have been scientifically endorsed by psychology, medicine, and social science. They are simple, yes, but they work!

Do it: Be positive, get more exercise, and eat better food. Why wouldn't you do it? You owe it to yourself.

Once you try it and start getting results over time, you'd be surprised to see how amazing life can be. You'll regret not doing these things sooner.

So what are you waiting for? Your new, stress-free life begins today.

Here's to a happier, more relaxed, and stress-free tomorrow!

Exclusive 5-day mindfulness course just for you!

We will be sharing how to get started on mindfulness, increase your self-awareness, inner peace and lower your anxiety levels and stress. Each day will involve actual practical steps that you can do at the comfort of your home!

Simply let us know where to send the course e-mails to via this link below.

https://bit.ly/miranda-yates

For any general feedback & enquiries, you can reach us at bookgrowthpublishing@mail.com

References

All images are courtesy of Pixabay.

American Academy of Dermatology. (2019). Feeling Stressed? How Your Skin, Hair And Nails Can Show It. ScienceDaily. https://www.sciencedaily.com/releases/2007/11/071109194053.htm

American Psychological Association. (2021). Stress effects on the body. Apa.org. https://www.apa.org/topics/stress/body

Bernstein, B. (2016, April 12). Financial Stress Is a Leading Cause of Divorce. EzineArticles. https://ezinearticles.com/?Financial-Stress-Is-a-Leading-Cause-of-Divorce&id=9382814

Brooks, M. (2020, August 10). These Foods Make Your Stress & Anxiety WORSE | BlackDoctor.org - Where Wellness & Culture Connect. BlackDoctor.org. https://blackdoctor.org/foods-that-cause-stress/

Bruce, J. T. (2015, June 17). How Food Affects Your Stress Levels—Both Good and Bad. SUCCESS. https://www.success.com/how-food-affects-your-stress-levels-both-good-and-bad/

Carlos, D. (2019, August 23). Feeling Stressed? Your Nails Can Show It. Sunday Edit. https://edit.sundayriley.com/how-does-stress-affect-nails/

Engelmann, J. (2018). japan: work related suicides 2018 | Statista. Statista; Statista. https://www.statista.com/statistics/622325/japan-work-related-suicides/

Exploring Your Mind. (2015, December 20). Stress and Poor Nutrition. Exploring Your Mind. https://exploringyourmind.com/stress-poor-nutrition/

Felman, A. (2020, March 12). Stress: Why does it happen and how can we manage it? Www.medicalnewstoday.com. https://www.medicalnewstoday.com/articles/145855

Frye, D. (2020, January 24). The Foods We Eat Do Affect Our Mental Health. Here's the Proof. | Psychology Today. Www.psychologytoday.com. https://www.psychologytoday.com/us/blog/evidence

-based-living/202001/the-foods-we-eat-do-affect-our-mental-health-heres-the-proof#:~:text=Yet%20the%20take-home%20message%20is%20clear%3A%20The%20foods

Hart, J. (2021). Stress Nutrition Advice - Nutritionist Resource. Www.nutritionist-Resource.org.uk. https://www.nutritionist-resource.org.uk/articles/stress.html#stressanddiet

Harvard Health Publishing. (2015, January 8). Best ways to manage stress - Harvard Health. Harvard Health; Harvard Health. https://www.health.harvard.edu/mind-and-mood/best-ways-to-manage-stress

HelpGuide. (2018, December 27). Burnout Prevention and Treatment. HelpGuide.org. https://www.helpguide.org/articles/stress/burnout-prevention-and-recovery.htm

Hogan, J. (2017, May 16). Stop Stress in Its Tracks with These 4 Quick and Clever Tricks. Verily. https://verilymag.com/2017/05/simple-ways-to-combat-stress

Horizon Clinics. (2020, December 21). Medically Reviewed Stress Management Techniques for Relief. Horizon

Clinics. https://horizonclinics.org/stress-management/

Hughes, L. (2017, March 2). How to Stop Feeling Anxious Right Now. WebMD; WebMD. https://www.webmd.com/mental-health/features/ways-to-reduce-anxiety

Humane Slaughter Association. (2019). Stress in Animals - Humane Slaughter Association. Hsa.org.uk. https://www.hsa.org.uk/stress-in-animals/stress-in-animals

Kaiser Foundation. (2021). Is stress harmful? It's all in the way you think about it – Insider. Kaiser Permanante. https://insider.kaiserpermanente.org/is-stress-harmful-its-all-in-the-way-you-think-about-it/

Kennard, J. (2008, June 10). A Brief History of the Term "Stress." Healthcentral.com; HealthCentral. https://www.healthcentral.com/article/a-brief-history-of-the-term-stress

Kilburn, M. (2019, June 11). What are your stress triggers? Www.avogel.co.uk. https://www.avogel.co.uk/health/stress-anxiety-low-mood/stress/what-are-your-stress-triggers/

Kollam, D. P. (2021, July 11). Why we are Stressed? Living in Well Being. https://www.livinginwellbeing.org/why-we-are-stressed/

Kramer, J. (2019, January 10). 7 Foods That Secretly Stress You Out. EatingWell. https://www.eatingwell.com/article/291444/7-foods-that-secretly-stress-you-out/

Krans, B. (2018, August 28). 16 Simple Ways to Relieve Stress and Anxiety. Healthline. https://www.healthline.com/nutrition/16-ways-relieve-stress-anxiety#3.-Light-a-candle

Link, R. (2018, January 7). 11 Signs and Symptoms of Too Much Stress. Healthline. https://www.healthline.com/nutrition/symptoms-of-stress#TOC_TITLE_HDR_4

Marksberry, K. (2011). What is Stress? - The American Institute of Stress. The American Institute of Stress. https://www.stress.org/what-is-stress

Mayo Clinic Staff. (2019, April 4). How Stress Affects Your Body and Behavior. Mayo Clinic; https://www.mayoclinic.org/healthy-lifestyle/stress-management/in-depth/stress-symptoms/art-20050987

Nazario, B. (2021, January 7). 10 Ways to Stop Stress Now. WebMD. https://www.webmd.com/heart-disease/heart-edu-20/stop-stress-now

NHS. (2021, February 1). 10 stress busters. Nhs.uk. https://www.nhs.uk/mental-health/self-help/guides-tools-and-activities/tips-to-reduce-stress/

NHS Scotland. (2018). Struggling with stress? Nhsinform.scot. https://www.nhsinform.scot/healthy-living/mental-wellbeing/stress/struggling-with-stress

Pietrangelo, A. (2017, June 5). The Effects of Stress on Your Body. Healthline. https://www.healthline.com/health/stress/effects-on-body#Respiratory-and-cardiovascular-systems

Scholle, A. (2015, July 7). 5 Ways to Relieve Stress. The Center for Mind-Body Medicine. https://cmbm.org/blog/5-ways-relieve-stress/

Scott, E. (2019). 10 Things to Stop Doing If You're Stressed. Verywell Mind. https://www.verywellmind.com/dealing-with-stress-10-things-to-stop-doing-3145265

Scott, E. (2020, September 17). The Link Between Stress and Hair Loss. Verywell Mind.

https://www.verywellmind.com/is-stress-a-cause-of-hair-loss-3144822

segal. (2017, December 31). Stress Symptoms, Signs, and Causes: Improving Your Ability to Handle Stress. Helpguide.org. https://www.helpguide.org/articles/stress/stress-symptoms-signs-and-causes.htm

Shafir, H. (2020, November 6). Eustress vs Distress: Positive & Negative Types of Stress. Choosing Therapy. https://www.choosingtherapy.com/eustress-vs-distress/

Shrout, R. (2018, November 13). What are the effects of stress on a relationship? University of Nevada, Reno. https://www.unr.edu/nevada-today/news/2018/atp-relationship-stress#:~:text=Stress%20is%20common%20in%20relationships.%20All%20couples%20experience

Soilson, J. A. (2015, September 28). Financial Stress and Divorce. Fitch Law Partners LLP. https://www.fitchlp.com/blog/2015/09/financial-stress-and-divorce/

UK Counselling Directory. (2015, November 23). Is stress a mental health problem? Www.counselling-Directory.org.uk. https://www.counselling-directory.org.uk/memberarticles/is-stress-a-mental-health-problem